THE CONCISE GUIDE TO SOUTH CAROLINA STATE GOVERNMENT

THE CONCISE GUIDE TO SOUTH CAROLINA STATE GOVERNMENT

VINCENT SHEHEEN

THE UNIVERSITY OF SOUTH CAROLINA PRESS

Published in association with
Parker Poe Adams & Bernstein LLP

© 2025 Vincent Sheheen

Published by the University of South Carolina Press
Columbia, South Carolina 29208

uscpress.com

Printed in the United States of America

Library of Congress Cataloging-in-Publication Data
can be found at http://catalog.loc.gov/.

ISBN: 978-1-64336-601-2 (hardcover)
ISBN: 978-1-64336-643-2 (paperback)
ISBN: 978-1-64336-644-9 (ebook)

Published with the generous support of Parker Poe Adams & Bernstein LLP, a law firm proudly serving the needs of business and government across South Carolina.

To my father, Fred Sheheen, who loved his family; cared deeply about his state; fully enjoyed politics; willingly took risks; fought as a happy warrior; took on unpopular causes; and believed public service was a privilege, duty, and honor. I couldn't have done any of it without you.

CONTENTS

List of Illustrations *ix*
Introduction *xi*

Chapter 1
A Very Short History: Why South Carolina's Government Is What It Is *1*

Chapter 2
The Legislative Branch: A History of Power *19*

Chapter 3
The Executive Branch: The Governor, a Growing Power *43*

Chapter 4
The Judicial Branch: A Nonpartisan Force *71*

Chapter 5
Important State Agencies: Meeting the Needs of a Growing State *91*

Chapter 6
Local Governments: A New Story for South Carolina *113*

Conclusion: A Continuing Journey *125*

Appendix. State Agencies *127*
Notes *135*
Works Consulted *141*
Index *143*
About the Author *151*

LIST OF ILLUSTRATIONS

Figure 1
Robert Smalls, 1870s   20

Figure 2
Solomon Blatt, 1967   24

Figure 3
Benjamin Tillman, ca. 1918   45

Figure 4
Richard Riley, ca. 1983   47

Figure 5
Jean Toal, 1979   72

Figure 6
Olin D. Johnston, 1956   92

Figure 7
Joe Riley, 1986   114

INTRODUCTION

South Carolina is too small for a republic, but too large for an insane asylum.
—James L. Petigru, 1860

The story of South Carolina's government is, in part, a story of its culture, and the story of its culture shapes the story of its government. And South Carolina's story has profoundly impacted the history and government of the United States itself. South Carolina's most prominent citizens have been leaders in times of war and peace, in the arts and the written word, and its cultural impacts, for good and for bad, are lasting.

South Carolina is a state of over five million people, was one of the first thirteen colonies, and has a unique history of self-government. South Carolina has a population comparable to that of the countries of Norway, New Zealand, or Costa Rica and a land mass significantly larger than Israel's or Switzerland's. Dramatically affected from its founding by the immigrant populations who arrived in the colony and by its conflicts with England, South Carolina's people and government have maintained a culture and governing structure that rejects centralization of power, whether it be in England, Washington, DC, or the South Carolina governor's office.

South Carolina's governing structure and civic norms have been forged in conflicted loyalties, intense division, a real sense of place, and a jealous guarding of independence. Its culture and government have been roiled by conflicts that arose with the Indigenous Americans who were in South Carolina first, its English rulers overseas, racial divisions created by the establishment of slavery, the Civil War,

Reconstruction's Black political empowerment, a White supremacist backlash, the industrialization of the South, the Great Migration, the civil rights movement, the emergence of Republican Party power, and a conflicted modernity. These same changes created a rich and diverse culture with implications far beyond the state's boundaries.

In recent times industrialization, population growth, and modernization have brought profound changes to South Carolina's state government structure. Yet no recent book or comprehensive text explains to its leaders, citizens, students, or scholars how and why the state government is structured and how it works. The last attempt to comprehensively explain South Carolina's state government operations occurred more than twenty years ago with the release of a short summary paperback titled *A Brief Guide to State Government in South Carolina*, written by Richard Young and published through the Center for Governance Institute, Institute of Public Affairs, at the University of South Carolina. Since that time much has changed in the state's governance and government, including tremendous changes in the executive branch positions that are elected, processes for appointments of many state agency heads, wholesale abolition and consolidation of major departments, and changes in the legislative branch's operations. In modern history, South Carolina has moved from a completely legislatively dominated state to a government with more balanced powers. These structural and political changes are not well documented or explained. Nor does any recent book explore and explain why South Carolina's system of government has evolved and changed to become what it is today.

The Concise Guide to South Carolina State Government briefly explains the historical roots of South Carolina's government structure, touching on major changes over time and providing a more detailed explanation of its current structure and operations. Trends, some of them laudable and some abhorrent emerge throughout the state's history and should become apparent throughout this book. These trends include the state's resistance to external authority, commitment to the legislature as the "people's branch" of government, historical enshrinement of White supremacy, continuation of geographical political divides, continued one-party dominance, and a rich blending of cultural milieus.

My hope is that leaders, citizens, students, and educators across South Carolina will use this book to understand how their government functions, how they operate within it, and how the search for a better government should be never ending. As an adjunct instructor of state government at the University of South Carolina Honor's College, I became frustrated that written discussions of South Carolina's government are woefully out of date and do not account for almost twenty years of changes in government structure and operations. This book is meant to fill that gap. My hope is that the interested reader will enjoy this book as an informative quick read or open it up as needed for easy reference. It should help the student, the teacher, the legislator, the staffer, the voter, the politician, the lobbyist, the businessperson, and others better understand how their government works.

From my late twenties until my late forties I served as a city prosecutor, a member of the South Carolina House of Representatives, and a state senator, serving on various committees and in numerous leadership positions. I was twice a major political party's nominee for governor and currently serve as mayor of one of our important cities. These roles gave me a look at the inner workings of politics, government, and decision-making. A vantage point of power opens an often-unseen view of how government works in actuality and not just in theory. I came away from my legislative service with the understanding that, although structure and formal power most certainly matter, even more often it is the character of individuals and their effective use of informal power that determines outcomes. Never to be lost in the discussion of government structure and actors should be that most mighty of motivators—public opinion—to which both government structure and individual leaders bend. For better or worse, a government is the embodiment of the wisdom of its people.

1

A Very Short History

Why South Carolina's Government Is What It Is

South Carolina's government has evolved over centuries from colonial times up to the present day. Sometimes change in government has been abrupt such as during the American Revolution, Civil War, Reconstruction, and the civil rights era. Oftentimes change came at an excruciatingly slow pace. South Carolina government is a reflection of its people and its history.

The Precolonial Period (1500s)

In the 1500s South Carolina was a sparsely inhabited region by modern standards, populated by small Native American tribes who likely arrived from Asia over thousands of years.[1] Their cultures were rich, varied, and ancient. Several modern nations and tribes, including the Catawba, Pee Dee, and Waccamaw, trace their ancestry back to those who populated the area at the time of the arrival of Europeans. Tribal names and languages also live on in the names of many rivers and regions of South Carolina, including the Catawba, Wateree, Pee Dee, and Enoree Rivers.

Spanish explorers arrived in the early 1500s, making landfall at Winyah Bay near Georgetown and finding the land of "Chicora" and the tribes who populated it. Soon one group of Spaniards enticed friendly Indigenous peoples aboard their ship, violently captured them, and sold them as slaves. One of the captives who was taken to Spain was given the name Francisco de Chicora. He worked as a guide for the Spaniards in the New World and ultimately escaped back to his people while acting as a guide near what would become Georgetown.[2] Perhaps Francisco de Chicora was the first North American to rebel against European rule?

After initial forays on the coast the Spaniards moved inward to the Indigenous American community of Cofitachequi, likely in the present-day Camden area on the Wateree River, just northeast of what would become the center of South Carolina. Here the explorer Hernando de Soto encountered the cacica ruler of Cofitachequi, who, the Spanish referred to as Cacica.[3] According to Spanish reports, the Cacica welcomed De Soto by removing a strand of pearls from her neck and placing them over his head. After a couple of weeks the Spaniards continued marching inland and took the cacica captive to accompany and guide them. She would quickly escape, setting another example of North Americans rebelling against European rule and embodying the human desire for freedom that would be exhibited many times by many people in the area.

In competition with the Spanish, the French shortly followed to the area. They established an outpost at what is today called Parris Island, now a major training facility for the United States Marines, in the Lowcountry of South Carolina. Religiously persecuted French Huguenot Protestants would later come to the region as well; this movement continued for almost one hundred years. These French Protestants would permanently grace the state with regional and landmark names such as Gervais, Huger, and Horry, all of which remain embedded in South Carolina's geography and culture to this day. The French and Spanish created a regional rivalry for control that was unsustainable and mutually defeating, and their influences soon virtually disappeared. The English saw an opportunity for expansion.

The Colonial Period and the Fundamental Constitutions (Early 1600s–Mid-1700s)

The English made forays into the Carolinas early in the 1600s at the beginning of what would become a world-changing British colonial empire. In 1663 King Charles granted a charter to eight of his royalist supporters making them "true and absolute lords and proprietors" of the Carolinas. Thus, a unique system of governance was established in North America: that of the eight Lords Proprietors.[4] This system was singular in colonial America and would have lasting and profound influences on the cultural and governmental development of South Carolina. Among the lords who "owned" the Carolinas were Edward Hyde, first Earl of Clarendon; John Berkeley, first Baron Berkeley of Stratton; Anthony Ashley Cooper, first Earl of Shaftesbury; and Sir John Colleton. Again, these are names that continue to mark South Carolina political subdivisions, rivers, and landmarks.

Notably Lord Ashley and his personal secretary, John Locke, who would become one of the most distinguished thinkers of the Enlightenment, drafted the Fundamental Constitutions of Carolina to ostensibly govern the colony. Although never formally adopted, the Fundamental Constitutions set forth a spirit of governance demonstrating how the Lords Proprietors thought about the colony. In the early years, the Fundamental Constitutions were cited by both the Lords Proprietors and colonists. The Fundamental Constitutions were perhaps the first written documents in the New World that provided for important fundamental rights such as voting by secret ballot, trial by jury, and protections for land ownership.[5] Most important for the independent spirit of the Carolinas, the Fundamental Constitutions created an expectation that laws must receive popular approval from the small settlement, allowing space for self-government from the start.

The document was also progressive in allowing for relative freedom of religion. The Lords Proprietors and the Fundamental Constitutions encouraged any and all possible settlers to come to the Carolinas, regardless of religion or country of origin. These settlers included French Huguenots, German religious dissenters, the Irish, the Welsh, and Jews.[6] The Fundamental Constitutions promised religious freedom to anyone who believed in God, becoming one of the first organizational documents to restrain government's influence over religion. People of all religions were welcomed, with the notable exception of Catholics, due to England's historic break with Rome and active anti-Catholic bias. Many of these new immigrants came as indentured servants, performing backbreaking work on plantations and in small businesses, bound to the landowners for a set number of years.

The Fundamental Constitutions also sought to guarantee every freeman "absolute power and authority over his negro slaves," a constitutional enshrinement with shattering consequences for the future of South Carolina and the nation. South Carolina became an English colony in North America in which slavery was established in a written document from the beginning.

The Carolinas were a popular destination for wealthy immigrants from the English colony of Barbados, a fact that was also critically important for the future cultural and political development of South Carolina and its government. These eager immigrants were looking for more land and more economic opportunity than their wealthy island colony could provide. Because of the strong Barbadian influence on its development, South Carolina has been sometimes referred to as a "Colony of a Colony." The White Barbadians brought a culture of commercial activity, the plantation economy, the use of slave labor, resistance to central government, and an independence of living that has had lasting effects on South Carolina's government and history and indeed that of the nation.[7] Three of South Carolina's early governors came from Barbados: Sir John Yeamans, James Colleton, and Robert Gibbes.[8] Yeamans was a colorful character who bankrupted his Barbadian estate, sought his fortune in the Carolinas, allegedly had his paramour's husband killed so he could marry her, scrambled into the governorship of the colony, and was accused of illegally profiting from the sale of foods while governor.[9]

Equally important to the future of South Carolina were the enslaved African people brought to the colony from the Barbados plantations. The first Africans in North America were brought to South Carolina, establishing the evil institution of slavery that would haunt the state for generations. Black Barbadians brought with them important cultural and economic resources, including agricultural technology and food preparation techniques that have lasted hundreds of years, and individual and societal survival techniques for living in a White supremacist system. The generations of British and African cultural combinations that followed would shape the state's social and political worlds and development of the nation's government, politics, music, art, literature, religion, and cuisine, creating a unique cultural blend. As Europeans and Africans populated the colony, the once robust Indigenous cultures shrank through disease, warfare, and forced westward movement.

A clash over systems of control quickly developed between the Lords Proprietors and the Barbadian merchants and plantation owners. Unlike most other colonies that were directly controlled by a European monarch or a single individual, the governor of South Carolina was appointed by the Lords Proprietors. Early government in colonial South Carolina was unified, with executive, legislative, and judicial functions overlapping and intermixed. The Lords Proprietors initially appointed a Grand Council that made most government decisions.[10] The council's authority included executive powers, rule-making powers, and even judicial powers to prosecute crimes. The Lords Proprietors allowed the establishment of a local parliament, the Commons House of Assembly, made up of prominent, elected local citizenry.[11] This parliament had frequent engagements and clashes with the governors and Grand Council, continuing to build distrust in the new colony against centralized authority.

The city of Charles Town quickly became the de facto center of the Carolinas and a commercial power in the New World, with a thriving commercial center, surrounding plantations, and a bustling seaport. For a period in the early 1700s the colony's waters were frequented by pirates such as Blackbeard and Stede Bonnet, the "gentleman pirate."[12] In 1718, Blackbeard captured a ship with several prominent South Carolinians aboard and used their captivity to blackmail the leaders of the city of Charles Town into providing him with supplies.

America's first colonial revolution occurred in 1719, when the parliament of South Carolina declared itself a convention of the people not beholden to the Lords Proprietors but loyal only to the king.[13] This Revolution of 1719 brought intermittent violence and protest until the Lords Proprietors relinquished control, empowering what had become the General Assembly. The colony's governor would henceforth be appointed directly by the king. South Carolinians enjoyed the taste of their first successful rebellion against central authority. In a foretaste of things to come the revolutionaries pledged to "choose an Assembly . . . and to support their representatives with their lives, and fortunes."[14] The South Carolina colonists' streak of independence and distrust of central authority would not be sated by these changes. For the next forty years the increasingly independent General Assembly would chip away at royal power and fight with a rotating cast of royal governors.

Meanwhile immigration continued, and populations grew with large influxes of Germans and even larger numbers of Scots-Irish to the "Backcountry" (inland South Carolina) in the middle 1700s. The forebears of Andrew Jackson and John C. Calhoun were among this wave of Scots—Irish settlers.[15] These Scots-Irish were truly Scots pushed out of Scotland by English power and starved out of Ireland by England's often cruel and domineering policies. They came to America understanding how to fight against authority and unafraid to do so. Their increasing numbers created a White majority population in the colony that lasted from the 1770s until 1820. South Carolina had a higher percentage of Scots-Irish than almost any other colony. This influx had a lasting influence on the society and norms of South Carolina. A trip to rural Scotland informs a visitor of how much traditional White South Carolinians' cultural aspirations are linked to that land and the close link in peoples, traditions, music, and food that still remains.

South Carolina's French population also grew. Facing discrimination and violence in Catholic France, numerous Huguenot Protestants came to the colony, with no other colony receiving as high a percentage of its population. And more Africans were kidnapped and brought into the colony to be enslaved on plantations, in homes, and in businesses.

As growth continued new tensions developed. The feisty newcomers of the Backcountry wanted power and influence that was begrudged by the old-guard center of power in Charles Town. Institutions of order, such as courts, churches, and law enforcement existed in the Lowcountry seats of power, but the Backcountry tended to make do on its own, with independent local militias called Regulators forming to enforce order.[16] It is thought that John C. Calhoun's father, Patrick Calhoun, was a Regulator leader.[17] Common-law marriages took place because of a lack of clergy, with Backcountry settlers once again making their own way. This necessity for self-reliance further solidified the culture of independence and distrust of central authority that had already become a defining characteristic of South Carolina culture.

By the 1760s, the Regulators were a powerful Backcountry force, Charleston was one of the leading cities in the Americas, the Established Church of England had rivals in the Backcountry Presbyterians and other dissenter sects, and South Carolina's General Assembly continued to be a power center for wealthy and influential colonists who wanted little interference from the king or British parliament. Political conflicts between the upstart Backcountry and traditional Lowcountry elite did not interfere with the White colonists' unified support of Black enslavement. The plantation economic system, transmuted from Barbados, had grown and developed in the colony, relying on enslaved labor to farm crops such as rice, tobacco, and indigo. The importation and reliance on the labor of enslaved Africans would, of course, have a tremendous influence on the development of culture, government, and the lives of all South Carolinians then and now.

American Independence and the Creation of the General Assembly (Late 1700s)

In the late 1700s, South Carolina's historic resistance to strong, centralized authority quickly led the colony to join the calls for independence that arose in the northern colony of Massachusetts. Arguably the economic model of South Carolina, so reliant on the export of raw agricultural goods, should have made it one of the last colonies to join the independence movement. Instead the South Carolina governing class's culture led to an early joining of that revolutionary effort. South Carolina's assembly declared a new constitution in early 1776, the second of the colonies to do so and the first in the South. While forming its own government the colony still recognized itself as an English dependent suffering "unhappy differences" from Great Britain.[18] But by 1778, South Carolina's break with Britain was complete, and the colony declared itself an independent nation governed, as it had so long asserted, by its own people. Notably the document disestablished the Anglican Church as the church of South Carolina.

Guerrilla warfare was perfected during the revolution in the Carolinas by former regulators and militia leaders such as Thomas Sumter, "the Gamecock," and Francis Marion, "the Swamp Fox." Their constant harassment of the British military eventually helped lead to the repulsion of Cornwallis's British forces from the state and British surrender to George Washington's army in Virginia.

South Carolina voted to adopt the United States Constitution in 1788 and became a part of the Union. Support for the United States Constitution was notably divided between the Backcountry settlers and Lowcountry gentry. Delegates from Charleston and surrounding areas voted overwhelmingly to adopt the federal constitution. Not so in the even more independent-minded Backcountry, where coffins were painted black and paraded through the dusty streets and buried as a symbol of the interment of liberty.[19]

The history and cultural distrust of central authority led the new state to create an extremely powerful General Assembly and weak governor. The General Assembly consisted of a House of Representatives and a Senate. The governor was entirely beholden to the General Assembly, whose members elected him to a limited two-year term. The position was little more than a figurehead and reward for good service.[20]

Black Resistance, Civil War, and a New Constitution (1800s)

By the early 1800s, the state's population was majority Black, reaching a high of 60 percent in 1880.[21] Adding to the various cultures of resistance to authority that had developed in South Carolina was perhaps the ultimate example of a culture striving for freedom: the numerous rebellions by enslaved Blacks fighting to be free. From the time of chattel slavery's establishment in the state, Black South Carolinians resisted enslavement, in some cases escaping to Spanish territory to the south and otherwise fighting to be free. These episodes of resistance struck fear in the minds of many White South Carolinians, and there were frequent rumors of planned Black uprisings and feared massacres of Whites. Well-known examples such as the Stono Rebellion in 1739, and the revolt led by Denmark Vesey in 1822, remind us that Black South Carolinians rebelled against unjust authority with active resistance.[22] But Blacks sought freedom in less violent ways as well. In 1818, Black members of Methodist churches that were controlled by Whites formed their own congregations in Charleston so that they could play roles of spiritual leadership in their own religious redemption.

The plantation system, reliance on enslaved labor, and shift to cotton as a primary crop meant that opportunities for poor Whites were limited, and a massive outward migration of White laboring families occurred to Western states. Between 1820 and the start of the Civil War, over 40 percent of all Whites born in South Carolina moved westward in search of opportunities that did not exist for them in South Carolina.[23] Future president Andrew Jackson perhaps typified this phenomenon; he grew up impoverished in the South Carolina Backcountry and moved to North Carolina and then to Tennessee.[24] At the same time, White farmers also moved westward taking their enslaved workforce with them in search of new lands on which to establish plantations.[25]

A short comparison of Andrew Jackson and John C. Calhoun is useful in demonstrating the two paths Backcountry Scots-Irish South Carolinians followed in relation to the new Union. Calhoun, who remained in the state, would serve in national office but become a preeminent anti-unionist and develop theories of nullification and succession, laying much of the philosophical groundwork for secession. Jackson left the state; fought the established political power structure in the United States; became president; and promoted increased national unity in a strong, more democratic, national government. When South Carolina threatened nullification and secession in the 1830s, Jackson famously stated that "to say that any State may at pleasure secede from the Union, is to say that the United States are not a nation." For good measure he added, "Tell them if one South Carolina finger be raised in defiance of this Government, that I shall come down there: and once I'm there, I'll hang the first man I lay hands on to the first tree I can reach."[26]

Ironically these two Scots-Irish South Carolina natives would serve for a term together as president and vice president. One went on to lay the foundations for the Civil War, while the other planted the seeds of robust democratic participation in an increasingly unified nation. Their competition reached a fever pitch in 1830 at the annual Jefferson Day celebration attended by then-President Jackson and then–Vice President Calhoun. That night President Jackson rose to give a toast, glowering at his vice president: "Our Union—it must be preserved." Calhoun raised his glass and drank and rejoined: "The Union. Next to our liberties, most dear."[27]

The division among the states leading up to the Civil War is a well-known and well-discussed subject. Also well-known is the leading role South Carolina played in agitating against and eventually leading the secession from the United States of America. South Carolina elites' cultural antipathy toward centralized power and their commitment to maintaining enslavement of African Americans paved the way for South Carolina to become the first state to secede from the Union and convince its fellow Southern states to follow the same destructive path. The state's "Declaration of the Causes of Secession" noted that the domestic institution of slavery must be preserved and castigated the free states for having "encouraged and assisted thousands of our slaves to leave their homes." South Carolina's attack on federal forces at Fort Sumter was a prelude to many bloody and devastating battles fought within the state. Change was coming and coming quickly.

The post–Civil War period had profound influences on South Carolina's culture and government, including the election of Black officials along with White Republicans. But first there was an attempt by the White Democratic elite to maintain control. Under President Andrew Johnson a state constitutional convention was called in 1865. According to historian Walter Edgar, "an observer would have thought he or she was taking a trip in a time machine. The state's antebellum elite dominated the proceedings."[28] Like the ones before it, the resulting constitution was not submitted to the people for ratification. And while the new constitution recognized the emancipation of the enslaved, it did little else to support their full citizenship. However the new constitution altered the political structure of the state, allowing the popular election of governors for four-year terms, giving governors the veto power, making new districts the basis for state House and Senate elections, and removing property qualifications for voting.[29]

Reconstruction, the Constitution of 1868, and
White Backlash (1867–95)

A few years later change of control in Washington produced astounding results in South Carolina. After Congress passed the Reconstruction Acts in 1867, more than 90 percent of eligible Black men registered to vote, and almost all of them went to the polls. Change in Washington then produced even more change in South Carolina. The goal of allowing freed Blacks the right to vote was not easy in coming, but in 1868 a state constitutional convention convened that included 124 persons, 73 of whom were Black and 51 of whom were White.[30] This constitution would be submitted to and approved by the people, with over 85 percent of Black registered voters participating. Over the next few years South Carolina would elect Joseph H. Rainey, the first Black man to be seated as a United States congressman; appoint a Black state supreme court justice and have numerous Black elected officials. The Constitution of 1868 allowed for all men to have the right to vote regardless of race, heritage, or property ownership. The Constitution of 1868 is *the only* South Carolina Constitution ever submitted in toto to the voters for approval.[31]

This constitutional effort of 1868 was important in its commitment to education, creating the separately elected superintendent of education and guaranteeing free public education to all South Carolina citizens. The document also empowered local county governments for the first time, taking steps away from the South Carolina tradition of state-level political dominance in favor of more local control. The new constitution also made changes to the structure of the branches of government. While maintaining the dominance of the General Assembly, the new constitution did make the governor popularly elected and vested the office with some new powers. This first step toward executive-branch independence would prove important over the next century and a half.

The Republican Party became the party of freed Black citizens and White transplants from the North, relying for votes on the Black majority population of South Carolina. Electoral districts were drawn to minimize White voting power, and many White South Carolinians "simply took a walk" from electoral politics.[32] Whites and Blacks tended to avoid each other in daily civic life, and de facto segregation became a norm in much of the state for the first time.[33]

Also to be profoundly important were the ultimately successful attempts by White landowners to regain control, and subsequently White rural populists' (so-called Reformers) efforts to wrest political dominance from the White elite (Conservatives). As we shall see those efforts resulted in the Constitution of 1895 enshrining the concepts of racial separation and White dominance. White dominance had of course been the pre–Civil War norm for hundreds of years; however legally enforced physical, racial separation was a new concept in the state.

During this period a contrast emerged in the view of centralized political power between the Black and White populations of South Carolina. Along with their own substantial local efforts, the African American population was reliant in large part upon support from the centralized federal government and military to quell White violence and racial suppression. The White population, which had just attempted to secede from the United States of America, pushed back hard against that same central authority.

During this reconstruction period, many White South Carolinians did not just sit back and accept the federal government's efforts to empower Black citizens with equal rights. Nor did most leading White South Carolinians accept Black political participation. At the end of the Civil War it was reported that there was "in South Carolina a more virulent animosity existing in the minds of the common people against the [federal] government and people of the North than in any other State."[34] Numerous instances of Whites attacking and killing newly freed Blacks were reported, with all-White planter-class juries failing to convict when or if charges were brought.[35] In this time period South Carolina also saw the emergence of local, paramilitary forces under the umbrella of the Ku Klux Klan, which took action against Blacks and any Whites who attempted to assist them in asserting economic or political power.[36] White political and paramilitary efforts across the state were organized and effective, resulting in failed efforts by the Reconstruction state government to exert control and order.[37]

The Samuel J. Tilden versus Rutherford B. Hayes presidential race of 1876 would prove decisive about whether South Carolina would embrace the centralized authority of the United States government or revert to its historical character of resistance against authority outside of its borders. Federal support of Southern Reconstruction was clearly waning. The state and federal elections of 1876 would help determine how White and Black South Carolinians would coexist for the next century: in equality or oppression.

During the same election period former Confederate General Wade Hampton ran as the Democratic candidate for governor against incumbent Republican Daniel Chamberlain. A native of Massachusetts, Chamberlain came to South Carolina soon after the war and shortly thereafter served as attorney general for the state. Hampton advocated the recruitment of Black citizens into the Democratic Party, promising to continue the reforms of the 1868 Constitution such as voting rights and free schools.[38] But it soon became clear that the Democratic Party would be the party of White people dedicated to enforcing White power. The run-up to the governor's race of 1876 was marked by White violence and intimidation aimed at suppressing Black voters and regaining total power. It was an intensely organized effort, especially in the Upcountry of South Carolina and has been likened to a popular uprising.[39] Over thirty Black citizens were murdered after riots in the Ellington area in Aiken County. Paramilitary Red Shirts marched through towns by torchlight in efforts to intimidate. Black militias fought back in places but were generally overwhelmed.

Federal soldiers eventually stepped in more forcefully, and little violence occurred on election day itself. However, voting irregularities were strongly suspected. Both sides claimed fraud. The election was deadlocked, throwing the choice of governor to the Republican-controlled General Assembly, whose members promptly elected Chamberlain governor. Wade Hampton then established a shadow government, which included a shadow General Assembly. The shadow government soon came to exercise real power, receiving tax dollars directly from White citizens in the state, while Chamberlain's government was starved of funds, demonstrating that the "power of the purse" matters.

Similarly, the presidential race of 1876 was deadlocked with a vote too close to tally because of twenty-two disputed electoral votes, including South Carolina's seven votes.[40] Finally a congressionally chosen committee awarded all twenty-two disputed votes to Republican Hayes, including South Carolina's votes. In a suspected arrangement Hampton and his allies did not dispute the allocation of South Carolina's votes. In fact, Hampton visited Hayes shortly after his inauguration. On April 3, 1877, the new president ordered federal troops to be withdrawn from South Carolina. One week later Chamberlain and his staff vacated the state capitol building, and Wade Hampton moved in. Before leaving, the doomed governor drafted a letter to Black and White Republicans of the state recognizing that without federal backing he lacked the ability to stay in office: "[I]f a majority of the people of a State are unable by physical force to maintain their rights, they must be left to political servitude."[41] South Carolina's short experiment of embracing centralized power, racial equality, and national authority was over.

Black elected officials were not long to remain in power either. And soon Black voters would be effectively disenfranchised. The reemergence of White control in South Carolina was initially led by the antebellum elite, perhaps best embodied by Wade Hampton. While firmly reestablishing White power in South Carolina the reemerging antebellum leadership, referred to as Conservatives or Bourbons, otherwise supported a mainly status quo approach.[42] Although glorifying the antebellum tradition and White supremacy, the Bourbon leadership attempted to portray itself as more than simple racists. For example, on Wade Hampton's elevation to the governorship he pledged that his victory was not one of party or race but of honest government.[43] And at first he was successful in appointing some Black officials and maintaining the progressive reforms of 1868. But those efforts were short-lived with Black voters becoming disenfranchised by the White minority through violence, voter suppression, and fraud.

In the 1880's the Conservatives clinging to the status quo were challenged by the rise of the White, rural, economically progressive, and violently racist movement led by Ben Tillman. This post-Reconstruction, post-Conservative effort was referred to as the "Reform" movement. The Reform movement was made up of mostly rural Whites who advocated for progressive government ideas such as increased support of colleges and support for rural farmers while at the same time enforcing violent and strict racial divisions and White dominance.[44] These rural upstarts were opposed by the conservative Bourbon leadership made up of the White, former landed aristocracy such as Wade Hampton.

Perhaps the most important element leading to Black disenfranchisement and denigration was the rise of Tillmanism and the Constitution of 1896. As a successful Backcountry farmer from the Edgefield District who ran into hard times, Tillman created a political empire by harnessing the national farmers' reform movement of the latter part of the 1800s and coupling it with the anti-Black backlash in the South. Tillman was elected governor in 1890, overthrowing the remnants of the conservative Bourbon elite that had governed South Carolina in the post-Reconstructions era. By this time Wade Hampton had been elected to the United States Senate (in 1878). In 1890, in a blunt show of force Ben Tillman and his allies blocked Hampton's reelection to the US Senate. Then Tillman almost single-handedly orchestrated the Constitutional Convention of 1895. Tillman and his "Reformers" dominated the Constitutional Convention, enshrining Black disenfranchisement, legally segregating the population, taking legislative control over local governments, creating new counties to account for a growing population, and mandating separate schools for Black and White children. These changes were adopted during the convention over the objections of the few elected Black delegates, including former Congressman and Civil War hero Robert Smalls. Jim Crow had come to South Carolina with a vengeance and used the consolidation of power in the state government to ensure no opposition could succeed.

The Modern Era (1900s)

As the nineteenth century ended, the rays of a modern era in South Carolina peeked through the clouds. The modern era saw the rise of an industrialized economy, originally based on the textile industry. The concomitant rise of a business class, national modernization of government, and an urbanizing state would profoundly affect the state's form of government and government operations.

In keeping with South Carolina's conflicting history of freedom and rebellion against oppression, the state played a prominent role in the civil rights movement of the mid-twentieth century. Black leaders such Septima Clark, the Reverend I. DeQuincey Newman, lawyer Matthew Perry, and student activist and later US Congressman James Clyburn were joined by thousands of others in the fight against the state's White, Jim Crow legal regime. The protests and battles included the imprisonment of the Friendship Nine lunch counter protestors in Rockhill in 1961 and the Orangeburg Massacre in 1968, which occurred when state troopers opened fire on college students protesting segregation.

Much of the vocal and consistent force behind the South Carolina civil rights movement arose on the campuses of Black colleges. What an irony that a forceful power in overturning White supremacy would come from institutions created because of the racial segregation laws of the state. US Congressman and former Majority Whip Jim Clyburn was a part of this effort and explains in his autobiography *Blessed Experiences*: "[It] must have been a worrisome message coming from the state's largest black college. Black men and women who demanded freedom on college campuses might also demand their full and equal rights as citizens once they left campus."[45]

Slowly, and over time, through the efforts of the Black civil rights movement, progressive White leaders, and federal government pressure, the Jim Crow restrictions of South Carolina's post-Reconstruction era were felled. However, the racial divide in voting patterns and partisan divisions has remained, albeit switching parties in affiliations. White voters now overwhelmingly favor Republican candidates, and Black voters now overwhelmingly favor Democratic candidates, regardless of the particular issues in a campaign. With the switching of voting patterns, the one-party Democratic state effectively became a one-party Republican state.

The modernization and increased homogenization of South Carolina has seen changes to government structure, making it more akin to the federal model: the emergence of a strong governor's office, the creation of numerous state agencies to tackle society's present complexities, and the increased influence of local governments. But change in South Carolina has not come easily.

2

The Legislative Branch

A History of Power

Brave, thoughtful, wild, kind, colorful, controversial, hateful, divisive, and fascinating political figures have populated South Carolina's government for centuries. For a variety of reasons political figures from this small state often reach national prominence, from the colonial era up to today. Many of the most interesting political figures populated the state's powerful General Assembly. Many notable state and national figures got their political starts in the General Assembly or its predecessor body, including John Rutledge, John C. Calhoun, Ben Tillman, Marion Gressette, Edgar Brown, Strom Thurmond, Fritz Hollings, Dick Riley—and recent national political players Mick Mulvaney, Nikki Haley, and Tim Scott. Before discussing the mechanics of the legislative branch in South Carolina it is worth exploring the lives of two such impactful, historical figures from different eras: Robert Smalls and Solomon Blatt.

Smalls and Blatt embody important inflection points in South Carolina's history during which dramatic change occurred, powers clashed, and the future was dramatically altered. They also represent the tremendous diversity of backgrounds, ethnicities, and experiences of the citizens and leaders who have made South Carolina's culture distinct. They were two unlikely leaders, one an enslaved Black man who fought his way to freedom, and the other a first-generation Jewish American of Eastern European descent. Both had tremendous effects on the government, culture, and development of South Carolina.

FIGURE 1. *Robert Smalls, 1870s. Library of Congress, Prints & Photographs Division, LC-DIG-cwpbh-03683.*

Robert Smalls: *Slave, Hero, Politician, Statesman*

On April 5, 1839, Robert Smalls was born into slavery in the City of Beaufort.[1] It was rumored that his father was likely also the man who held him in slavery, John McKee, or McKee's son Henry, a circumstance that was not unusual in antebellum South Carolina. Regardless of his parentage, the McKee family seemed to favor Smalls over other enslaved children at the home.

They favored Smalls to such an extent that his mother worried her son would fail to understand the horrors of slavery. So she frequently sent him to the fields to watch other slaves beaten at the whipping post. Smalls developed a defiance to the institution of slavery and its social constructs and limitations. After a rebellious childhood Smalls moved to Charleston where McKee rented him out to work during his late teenage years; one such job was at the harbor.

Smalls ultimately found himself serving on a wooden steamship, the *Planter*. Early on the *Planter* hauled cotton along the coast as part of that lucrative trade. During this time Smalls learned much about the waterways on the South Carolina coastline and became a skilled navigator. When the Civil War broke out, Smalls continued his work on the *Planter*. By this time the Confederate Army used the *Planter* to supply military island encampments while avoiding the Union blockades set up outside Charleston Harbor. The overwhelmingly White crew was assisted in its work by eight enslaved people, including the twenty-two-year-old Smalls. Due to his knowledge of the waterways Smalls was often tasked with piloting the ship and was known as a "wheelman." For the war effort, the *Planter* had been outfitted with an arsenal of weapons to defend against Union attack, including a howitzer, pivot gun, and necessary ammunition.

On the night of May 12, 1862, Captain Charles Rylea and the White crew of the *Planter* made a fatal error, an error that Smalls had been anticipating and waiting for. That night against protocol the crew disembarked, leaving only their trusted and expert navigator, Smalls, and his fellow enslaved sailors onboard. For weeks Smalls had planned for just such an opportunity. He quickly briefed the other enslaved men about his plan to steal the *Planter*, join the Union effort, and gain his freedom. Two chose to stay behind, likely fearing for their safety, while Smalls and the others began a daring effort, knowing failure meant death or worse.

At 2 a.m., Smalls put on Captain Rylea's straw hat, instructed his meager crew to raise the Confederate and South Carolina flags, and left the dock. Daringly Smalls stopped at another wharf to pick up his wife and child, along with a few other brave escapees he had notified. Leaving the harbor in the dark of night Smalls boldly passed by Confederate Fort Johnson and blew the ship's whistle signaling that all was well. He did the same about an hour later while sailing past Fort Sumter. Smalls even mimicked the standing posture of Captain Rylea as the ship passed by the forts.

As the *Planter* approached the Union ships blockading the harbor, Smalls and his brave little crew removed the ship's flags and hoisted a white sheet. Robert Smalls delivered the ship, guns, and now former slaves to the Union. And he won freedom for his family.

Robert Smalls's amazing feats did not stop with his capture of the *Planter* and escape to freedom. He quickly joined the Union war effort, recruited Black soldiers to the army, piloted the *Planter* for the Union, engaged in numerous military actions including a Union assault on Fort Sumter, and ultimately became captain of the *Planter*. In an amazingly well-earned turn of fate Smalls stood on the deck of the *Planter* in Charleston Harbor during a ceremony marking the end of the Civil War in April 1865.

Unlike Cincinnatus, the famed Roman general, Robert Smalls did not retire upon completing his military career. Instead he settled in Beaufort, bought the house of his former enslaver, became a businessman, and ran for political office, endeavoring to help remake South Carolina. His career spanned the high-water mark of Black freedom and power during Reconstruction, as well as the cruel retrenchment of White backlash and power that followed.

Smalls was a founder of the Republican Party in South Carolina and loyally supported it his entire life. In 1868, he was a delegate to the state constitutional convention and supporter of its progressive ideas. In the early 1870s, Smalls won office in the South Carolina Senate and was elected as one of the first Black United States congressmen from South Carolina in 1874. But as White citizens began to reassert power and the Democratic Party took back state control, Smalls ran into trouble. In 1877, he was convicted in a bribery scandal, which was likely part of the campaign to remove Black officeholders. Nevertheless he was subsequently pardoned in an amnesty deal involving Republican and Democratic offenders. Amazingly he was reelected to Congress off and on until 1885 when Democratic control of the state solidified.

Perhaps saddest of all, Smalls's last political role was as one of only six Black members of the 1895 Constitutional Convention, a convention called for, enabled, and orchestrated by "Pitchfork"

Ben Tillman. In that role Smalls unsuccessfully fought against the disenfranchisement of Black South Carolinians. The new world he had dared to build, fought for, and campaigned for had come to an end—at least during his lifetime. At the Constitutional Convention of 1895, Smalls shamed the White members present stating "My race needs no special defense. . . . All they need is an equal chance in the battle of life."

Solomon Blatt: *A Life of Opportunity, Power, and Contradiction*

Solomon Blatt exercised more political power, for a longer period of time, than any other state legislator in South Carolina's history.[2] Blatt served as South Carolina Speaker of the House for more than thirty years, and he is an example of the polyglot nature of political figures in South Carolina. Rising to power in the early and mid-twentieth century Blatt was not the stereotypical White Anglo-Saxon Protestant plantation owner steeped in antebellum heritage. Nor was he the prototypical White rural country bumpkin so often portrayed in movies and on television. He was a complicated figure at the intersection of South Carolina heritage and history.

Blatt was born in 1896 to Orthodox Jewish immigrants who had left behind the pogroms and violence of czarist Russia and settled in small-town South Carolina in hope of a better life. Like so many Jewish, Lebanese, and Greek immigrants in the South at the time, Blatt's parents ran a small store. Blatt's father disembarked at Ellis Island in 1893, and unable to speak much English, made his way to Charleston with the help of Jewish contacts. There he was outfitted with a 125-pound peddler's pack and began to walk the rural countryside selling socks, combs, brushes, and all manner of sundries while sleeping under the stars. Eventually the senior Blatt could afford to bring his wife and growing family to America and opened a small store in rural Barnwell County. The family was fiercely thankful for the opportunities they found in the United States.[3]

FIGURE 2. *Speaker of the House Solomon Blatt calls to order a 1967 legislative session. Photograph by Vic Tutte. Copyright © The State Media Company. All rights reserved. For more information, contact the Walker Local and Family History Center at Richland Library, Columbia, SC 29201.*

Growing up Solomon Blatt engaged in the normal pursuits of the era including baseball, school, and work. But as a Jew among an overwhelmingly Christian population, he was aware of his differences. Blatt attended the University of South Carolina and its law school, eventually returning home to join a small law firm. But first the United States military sent him to the battlefields of World War I France for almost a year, where he witnessed the end of that great conflict.

Blatt worked as a practicing attorney all his professional life. In 1930 he ran for the South Carolina House of Representatives and lost in the Democratic primary, which was the deciding election in South Carolina since no Republican candidates could get elected in the "solid South." Blatt felt strongly that his Jewish heritage had weighed down his campaign. But in 1932, he again ran for the House, this time with the support of the local power structure, which assured his success.

Within several years of his election the South Carolina House selected Blatt as Speaker pro tempore, and in 1937, the House elected him Speaker, against the wishes of Governor Olin D. Johnston. Blatt served in the South Carolina House for fifty-three years, thirty-two of them as Speaker. His legislative service, from 1932 until 1986, spanned monumental changes in South Carolina and the world, including the Great Depression, World War II, the modernization of government, the civil rights era, and the Vietnam War.

Blatt was progressive on many economic issues, supporting increased taxation for education, creation of the technical college system, vast road improvements, investments at the state mental health hospital, and the creation of educational television. He also took great pride in the fact that Jews were so well accepted in South Carolina that the son of Russian Jewish immigrants could ascend to the heights of power. Publicly he rarely encountered overt discrimination, yet it was not absent. A notable example was a newspaper editorial written in 1938 that referred to him as the "Barnwell Jew." The editorial caused much outrage among Blatt's legislative supporters and friends, leading in part to a positive vote on a South Carolina House "Resolution of Confidence" for Blatt.

Although Blatt took such satisfaction in the integration of Jews into South Carolina's political system, he was reactionary toward the equality of Black citizens, proving once again that racism is not the sole province of any particular heritage. Blatt opposed Black integration in general, and he fought school integration with particular vehemence. While advocating against an integrated law school Blatt said, "The white people of South Carolina need not have any fear. . . . The Board of Trustees will do everything in their power to maintain the University of South Carolina for white students only, and in doing so, will protect the other institutions for white students." Blatt's opposition to integration remained strong, long past the time that most elected officials in South Carolina's leadership made peace with it.

In many ways Solomon Blatt lived and was an example of the American Dream in all its splendor. But he also voiced and fought for its worst prejudices.

Why Legislative Dominance Lasted for So Long in South Carolina

Generations of leaders in South Carolina have distrusted central authority all the way back to the time of the state's English settlement. Layer upon layer of political and cultural accretions solidified opposition to the very ideas of strong government and the centralization of governmental power. The Fundamental Constitutions of the Carolinas created by John Locke for use by the Lords Proprietors were an early attempt to check the use of governmental power against its free citizens. The independent commercial spirit of the early British immigrants from Barbados brought another anticentralized government influence to the colony. The South Carolina colonists' eventual conflicts with the Lords Proprietors and the successful Revolution of 1719 formalized this distrust of concentrated power when the colonists declared themselves "A Convention of the People." Finally the colony's willingness to defy the British king and Parliament during the American Revolution led it to adopt a form of government that empowered the "peoples' branch" of government above all other government powers. The General Assembly was considered the people's branch, and it would be the overwhelmingly dominant political force in the state for almost two hundred years.

This assertion of legislative dominance over the executive and judicial branches began early in the history of South Carolina. The first House of Assembly was allowed by the Lords Proprietors in 1671. It quickly became the most important political body for colonists. Following the revolt of 1719, the "Convention of the People" rejected the governor appointed by the lords and offered the governorship to James Moore Jr., hero of the colony's attacks against Indigenous tribes who lived on lands desired by colonists.[4] The Convention then formed the Commons House of Assembly to effectively exercise all political power in cooperation with Governor Moore. It became the political force in the colony that would-be leaders desired to join, and the House exercised great influence on the affairs of the colony. South Carolinians also petitioned the British Parliament to allow the colony to become a royal colony with increased self-sovereignty directly under the king. Above all the colony made it clear that it would push back against management of its affairs from a faraway central government. In the years to come South Carolina frequently did so—against the British king, Parliament, US president, and Congress.

As colonial relations with Great Britain dramatically deteriorated throughout the colonies, a Mass Meeting of South Carolina leaders was called in December of 1773.[5] The mass meeting laid the groundwork for a totally independent government in South Carolina, eventually leading to the creation of a provincial congress to govern South Carolina by July 1775. Again and again the power of government in South Carolina rested with elected legislative bodies. In March 1776, months before the Declaration of Independence, South Carolina's provincial congress drafted a constitution for the colony.[6] It provided a governmental framework to operate the colony "until an accommodation of the unhappy differences between Great Britain and America can be obtained." On March 26, 1776, the South Carolina Provincial Congress adjourned itself and reassembled as the First General Assembly of South Carolina, consisting of a House of Representatives and a Senate. The South Carolina House elected the upper chamber from its own membership, and the two chambers jointly elected the president of South Carolina and other statewide offices. In other words, the Commons House of Assembly selected the members of all other branches of government. During this brief period South Carolina was in essence an independent nation governed only by itself. It would try this model out again to great disaster almost one hundred years later.

The break with Great Britain being conclusive, the legislature adopted another, permanent, constitution in 1778. This one created a true bicameral legislative body with a separately elected House of Representatives and Senate.[7] The chief executive's powers made that position a simple figurehead. A constitutional revision in 1790 brought the state into conformity with the new federal constitution, altered the size of the South Carolina House, confirmed Columbia as the capital, firmly established legislative dominance, and created twenty-two counties for courthouse jurisdictions.[8]

The historical establishment of a politically dominant General Assembly continued, with alterations, through the antebellum era, the Civil War, Reconstruction, and the first half of the twentieth century. Legislative dominance consistently survived for hundreds of years through successive governments of varying philosophies and political makeups. It was sustained during the brief political empowerment of Black freemen in Reconstruction, and it survived the White backlash of Tillman's reformers and the Jim Crow regime. A more balanced sharing of power between the three branches of government came only in the latter part of the twentieth century with the rise of popular governors, a robust business community, centralization of populations in cities, multiple efforts to make the state government look more like the federal government, and a strong executive branch.

Since the 1970s, the General Assembly has voluntarily (albeit often grudgingly) given up tremendous power, both to local governments and to the governor's office. Led by legislator and future governor John C. West of Camden, major changes to the constitution and statutory laws of the state occurred during the late 1960s and early 1970s, allowing for more local government control. And since 1994, the legislature has given the governor control of almost every state agency in South Carolina either through direct appointment of the director or through appointment of a governing board. State agencies will be discussed in more detail in chapter 5. Some agencies, such as the Department of Commerce and the Department of Social Services, have directors appointed directly by the governor. These types of agencies are considered part of the governor's "cabinet."[9] The governor exercises control over most of the remaining agencies by appointing the boards or commissions that govern them. Before 1994, many of these agencies were governed by boards or commissions appointed in part or in full by the legislative bodies.

Facilitated in large part by reapportionment requirements under the Federal Voting Rights Acts, the 1970s and '80s saw the election of significant numbers of African American members to the General Assembly. At the same time the General Assembly experienced a dramatic decline in Democratic members and a concurrent massive increase in Republicans. Federal reapportionment requirements also led to the stripping of representation from rural areas and a reallocation to urban areas.

Over successive years the General Assembly gave up appointment powers in favor of the governor's office, recently including control of appointments for the Department of Transportation. Advocates' justification for these changes has been the goal of better and more accountable governmental agencies. Whether these changes have resulted in the better or worse functioning of state government is much debated.

Recently the Government Restructuring Act of 2014, a bill introduced by the author of this book while he was in the South Carolina Senate, further empowered the governor's office. Among other changes, this act created the Department of Administration, disassembling the once powerful Budget and Control Board. The act also created mechanisms for the General Assembly to provide orderly oversight and investigation of the more powerful and independent executive branch and its agencies to achieve true checks and balances. Legislative oversight of the executive branch remains extremely difficult for a part-time legislature and should not be compared to the constant and robust oversight on the national level.[10]

As mentioned above the General Assembly also shed power, beginning in the 1970s, by allowing the creation of county governments and vesting the counties with certain authority and powers. This phenomenon will be discussed in chapter 6, on local governments in South Carolina.

The General Assembly in the Modern Era

Article III of the South Carolina Constitution sets forth the powers, duties, and responsibilities of the "legislative department." All legislative power is specifically vested in two "distinct branches." One "to be styled the 'Senate' and the other the 'the House of Representatives,' and both together the 'General Assembly of the State of South Carolina.'" Appropriately for the history of the state, the legislative framework laid out in the constitution comes before that of the executive branch in Article IV and the judicial in branch in Article V; the South Carolina House of Representative was created first within the legislative branch. And the General Assembly is tasked to "frequently assemble for the redress of grievances and for making new laws, as the common good may require."

Legislation is required to be introduced by a member of the General Assembly, given three readings in each house, voted on positively during at least two readings in each house, and sent to the governor for consideration. Most legislative proposals also spend a lengthy amount of time in and receive consideration going through the committee processes of each body.

As in most states the General Assembly members are considered to be part-time, with the vast majority of members holding full-time jobs or being in retirement. Because they are part-time, legislators are very dependent on information and implementation of policies on leaders in the other two branches of government, which over time have all become full-time positions.

The General Assembly goes into full meetings of each chamber on Tuesdays, Wednesdays, and Thursdays of their operating sessions, which last from the second Tuesday in January until the second Thursday in May. Sessions may be extended by a supermajority vote of each body. During normal sessions the legislators debate bills, consider appointments from the governor, receive guests, send bills to committees, and take up other matters. The South Carolina Senate votes by voice, while the South Carolina House usually uses an electronic voting system.

The bodies differ notably in operation, with the Senate usually being a quieter place of deliberation where senators are required to be seated at their desks and are sent from the chamber by the sergeant at arms if their side conversations become too loud. The House is more boisterous with members wandering the aisles, negotiating with one another, and constantly engaging in small talk. In the

Senate male members are required to keep their coats on, while in the House men often leave them hanging from their chairs.

The South Carolina House of Representatives operates essentially without a filibuster system, while the South Carolina Senate has maintained some semblance of a filibuster for members who find themselves in the minority on any given issue. Each chamber elects its own clerk, sergeant at arms, reading clerk, and chaplain. Tone and tradition create different dynamics in each body and differences in the ways that members consider legislation, interact with each other, and reach decisions.

House of Representatives

Knowledge of operations of the state House of Representatives, its committee structure, and the workings within each committee is a powerful tool for legislators, lobbyists, and citizens for effectuating or stymying change. Like that of the United States government, South Carolina House of Representatives members are elected to a two-year term. Members must be twenty-one years of age and residents of the district they represent. The body consists of 124 members, who are supposed to be apportioned throughout the state based on census figures. The State Constitution guarantees at least one member to each county to ensure representation for small communities. However in 1964, the United States Supreme Court effectively outlawed this protection for small communities by ruling that the US Constitution requires representation based on strict proportionality regardless of whether a county is deprived of resident representation or not.[11] Therefore in South Carolina, as in some other states, the state constitutional requirement of at least one legislator per county is no longer enforced, depriving many small communities of resident representation. House members currently represent approximately forty-one thousand people per district, and this number is adjusted following each decennial census. House members do not pick their chamber seat assignments on the basis of party but instead upon their county of residence, allowing for a physical intermixture and socialization between the political parties.

Like the United States House, the South Carolina House is where all matters of appropriation and revenue raising must first be introduced. In joint sessions, the state House and Senate meet together in the House Chamber to jointly elect judges, university trustees, and a few other important state officers.

Organization

Traditionally legislative bodies in the United States are organized either along partisan lines or by seniority or some combination of both. The South Carolina House of Representatives is formally organized by neither. Instead its formal structure has evolved based on two main elements: committee structure and the position of Speaker of the House. This lack of formal partisan or seniority organization does not mean those factors do not matter. Indeed they have tremendous influence on legislative matters and outcomes. But unlike the state Senate or the United States Congress, nowhere are party or seniority mentioned in the house rules or its statutory authority as organizational principles.

The Speaker

Interestingly the organization of the South Carolina House of Representatives is left completely up to the House itself. The State Constitution creates no officers or structure at all. Instead the Rules of the House of Representatives and its traditions determine its operations. The very first rule of the SC House of Representatives creates the powerful position of Speaker of the House. The Speaker is to be elected on the first day of a session by the members of the State House.

Unlike in the United States House, Speakers are not chosen solely by the majority caucus. There is no legal requirement that the Speaker come from the majority party; however, for obvious reasons, a member of the majority party is elected Speaker, albeit with coalitions of support that often include minority members. This ability to build coalitions across party lines has given minority party members and their constituents some meaningful role in the selection of leadership, a minority role that does not exist presently on the federal level. Similarly the coalition building that occurs in electing a

Speaker lends itself to bipartisan relationships and goodwill between members.

The House rules and statutory laws vest the Speaker with tremendous power. The Speaker appoints committee members, presides over the body, and assigns legislation to committees. Subsequently enacted statutory authority designates the Speaker as the "chief administrative officer" of the House, giving the Speaker power over employee hiring, firing, and compensation as well as other business operations of the body. Between the rules and statutory authority, the Speaker can operate as a dominant force in the House. The Speaker also appoints numerous members of legislative and quasi-legislative boards and commissions such as the Joint Bond Review Committee (which reviews state bond matters and capital improvements), the Conservation Bank (which funds land conservation), the Judicial Merit Selection Commission (which screens judicial candidates), and many other similar bodies.

In particular, the dual ability to appoint state House committee members and assign legislation to House committees allows a Speaker to play an outsized role within the legislative and budget-making process. For example the Speaker can effectively determine who will chair a committee by appointing members to the committee who will vote for the Speaker's desired chair. Speakers can also often determine whether legislation will be positively recommended by a committee or die a slow death in a committee's closet simply by which committee to which they assign it. Furthermore legislators' desires to serve on meaningful committees gives an astute Speaker tremendous influence over each legislator as matters important to the Speaker are considered.

While not operating on a formal or strict seniority system, as the state Senate does, House traditions do reward seniority. For at least the last half-century, the Speaker of the House has been a seasoned legislator, working his way up through committee assignments and formal positions of authority such as committee chair or Speaker Pro Tempore.

The rules also create the position of Speaker Pro Tempore, which is again elected by the members of the House. The Speaker Pro Tempore's sole role is to preside over the House debate in the absence of the Speaker. Any further meaningful role played by the Speaker Pro Tempore depends entirely upon his or her relationship with the Speaker and the willingness of the Speaker to include him or her in leadership matters.

Legislative Committees

The legislative operation of the South Carolina House of Representatives is largely based on committee structure. The two most powerful permanent standing committees are the Ways and Means Committee and the Judiciary Committee. These two committees handle what are usually the most important legislative matters coming before the legislature. The Ways and Means Committee considers the multibillion-dollar annual budget and all matters falling within the budgeting and expenditure powers of the state. The Judiciary Committee considers changes to the State's civil and criminal legal system.

Other standing committees are:

- Agriculture, Natural Resources, and Environmental Affairs
- Education and Public Works
- Invitations and Memorial Resolutions
- Labor, Commerce, and Industry
- Legislative Ethics
- Medical, Military, and Municipal Affairs
- Operations and Management
- Oversight
- Rules

The topic areas of most of these committees are self-explanatory. Notably important has been the recent emergence of the powerful Oversight Committee. Created as part of the Restructuring Act of 2014, the Oversight Committee reviews operations of specific state agencies on a regular basis to investigate efficacy, waste, functionality, deficiencies, and successes. Before 2014, no legislative committee regularly reviewed the operations and efficacy of state agencies and programs.[12]

Most committees meet regularly during the legislative session to consider legislative proposals and other matters within their purview. Members serve on only one major standing committee but are also allowed to serve on the Legislative Ethics, Rules, Operations and Management, Oversight, or Invitations and Memorial Resolutions Committees. The Ethics Committee provides ethics rules interpretations for members and in conjunction with the State Ethics Commission considers ethics complaints made against members.

In the House of Representatives, committee members elect the chairs of each committee, who hold great power in setting the agenda and determining which bills come up for consideration and which bills are never heard from again. In rare circumstances, a truculent chair can be overridden by the committee members or even by the House as a whole, who by majority vote can require that legislation be considered. The chair of Ways and Means can exert tremendous control, effectively writing the vast bulk of the state budget before it is considered by any other members of the committee or House members.

Senate

The South Carolina Senate's members are elected to coterminous four-year terms and run on the same election cycle as the president of the United States. The state Senate consists of forty-six members who must be at least twenty-five years of age and residents of the districts they represent. Besides normal legislative matters, the state Senate gives advice, consent, and confirmation on most of the significant appointments made by the governor. Because the Senate's power is diffused between members to a greater degree than in the House, a working knowledge of Senate rules can be a huge asset for members and interested persons.

Under the state constitution, senators are supposed to be allocated as one member for each county to represent the varied geographical, population, and cultural differences of the state. As mentioned above, in 1964 the United States Supreme Court effectively outlawed legislative bodies that were created to, in part, protect small communities, requiring instead that representation be based on strict proportionality regardless of whether a county is deprived of resident representation or not. This US Supreme Court decision concentrated political power in the most populous areas, stripping power and the resources that follow from rural and small communities. Therefore in South Carolina as in some other states, the state constitutional requirement of one senator per county is no longer enforced, concentrating representation in urban areas. Rural senators now sometimes represent four or five counties and dozens of towns, while urban counties may have four or five resident senators, and large cities have numerous senators as advocates. In 2023, each senator represented approximately 111,000 citizens, and this number is adjusted every ten years based upon the census.

The rules and traditions of the state Senate are designed to force compromise. The Senate has a filibuster rule that allows a single senator to debate a bill for as long as that senator desires, until and unless cloture is invoked by the membership to end the debate. Traditionally members have been reticent to invoke cloture, although that reticence has waned somewhat as hyperpartisan affiliation has become more paramount than traditional Senate customs. Still on close and controversial issues the filibuster continues to act as a vehicle for compromise, forcing opposing positions to give and take to pass legislation. Partially the power of the filibuster remains due to the respect that members of the majority on an issue extend to the minority and the minority's willingness not to abuse the procedure.

Another important distinction between state House and Senate rules is the ability of any individual senator to block a bill from consideration. Within some limitations senators can make a notation that they are "desiring to be present." This blocking maneuver stops a bill from being considered but can be overridden by special vote of the Senate. The ability to block bills empowers individual senators and again often forces compromise by the proponents and opponents of legislation.

The Senate's many other rules and traditions have developed over time to preserve the individual power of separately elected senators while at the same time forcing compromise on disputed issues. For example if a senator states in the chamber that a proposed gubernatorial appointee is "personally offensive," then the appointee will not be approved by the other senators out of respect for the offended senator. This tradition is very rarely invoked and so remains respected by the body. Often the Senate temporarily adjourns debate on controversial bills while a small number of proponents and opponents sits down at a table or in a corner to discuss possible compromises, which they ultimately present to the full body.

Organization

The South Carolina Constitution allows the state Senate to organize itself as it sees fit. The rules of the Senate set out its organizational structure. Unlike in the House, the Senate's power is diffused among different positions, and individual senators retain significant institutional power.

For most of its history, the South Carolina Senate was strictly organized by the seniority system. A seniority system helps preserve individual power of each senator rather than vesting power in figures such as a Speaker or president. Historically members chose their seats, selected their committee assignments, became chairs of committees, and served in leadership positions based solely on their time of uninterrupted service in the Senate. Under this pure seniority system, internal fights for power were limited, and power and influence were gained by the length of a senator's service and the talents the senator brought to bear.

The strict seniority system was modified in 2000 when Republicans took a majority of seats and reorganized the Senate. Under the new system, the state Senate is organized under a mixed model based on political affiliation and seniority. Committee membership is allocated along majority and minority parties, and within those allocations seniority controls. Chairs of committees are reserved for majority members and are then allocated by seniority. Committee chairs often share subcommittee assignments with both majority and minority members.

As required by a recently adopted constitutional amendment, the Senate was reorganized again in 2018, removing the lieutenant governor as presiding officer and filling the presiding role with the president of the Senate. Perhaps ironically the last independently elected lieutenant governor of South Carolina, Henry McMaster, ultimately became governor when his predecessor, Nikki Haley, resigned the governorship to accept federal office.

The president of the Senate is elected by a majority of the Senate members. Like the Speaker of the House, successful presidents of the Senate often build coalitions of both Democrats and Republicans to win their positions. Unlike the Speaker of the House, the president's powers are limited. Presidents have no control over who serves on Senate standing committees or over the committee process. Presidents do preside over Senate debates, assign bills to committee, and appoint members and laypersons to several joint commissions. Furthermore some procedural motions are only allowed to be made by the president during the Senate's debates. Over recent years the Senate has also seen an informal custom develop that empowers the partisan majority leader to control the period set aside for motions to be made from the floor each day.

Committees

As in the House the legislative operation of the South Carolina Senate is largely based on committee structure. An important difference is that members self-select which committees they want to serve on within the partisan allocations. Another important difference is that the most senior member of the majority party serves as chair of each committee. These two differences help to reduce the centralization of power that occurs in the House. A Senate committee chair maintains significant power to set the agenda and determine whether a bill will successfully pass through the committee process.

As in the House, the two most powerful permanent standing committees are the Finance Committee and the Judiciary Committee. The Finance Committee considers the multibillion-dollar annual budget, which originates in the House, and all matters falling within the budgeting and expenditure powers of the state. The Finance Committee chair, with the help of staff, exercises independent power in initially drafting the state budget, similar to the power exercised by the House Ways and Means chair. The Judiciary Committee considers changes to the state's civil and criminal legal system and examines most appointments made by the governor before they go to the Senate floor.

Other standing committees are:

- Agriculture and Natural Resources
- Banking and Insurance
- Corrections and Penology
- Education
- Ethics
- Fish, Game, and Forestry
- General Committee
- Interstate Cooperation
- Invitations
- Labor, Commerce, and Industry
- Medical Affairs
- Operations and Management
- Oversight
- Rules
- Transportation

The topic areas of most of these committees are self-explanatory. Notably more committees exist in the Senate than in the House. The increased number of committees allows for an increased number of staff members who often develop more subject-matter expertise in particular areas. Again the Restructuring Act of 2014 gave momentum to creating a Senate Oversight Committee, which reviews operations of specific state agencies on a regular basis to investigate efficacy, waste, functionality, deficiencies, and successes.

Another key difference from the House is that Senate members serve on four substantive committees as well as some minor committees. And every member is guaranteed a spot on either the Judiciary Committee or the Finance Committee. Serving on multiple committees and having a spot on one of the two most important committees empowers individual senators. Most committees meet regularly during the legislative session to consider legislative proposals and other matters within their purview. Because senators serve on multiple committees and subcommittees, members are often seen darting throughout the Senate office complex attempting to attend meetings that are held simultaneously or close in time.

Agencies Directly Controlled by the Legislature or Shared Governance

Although the General Assembly has given up most of its historic power to directly control state agencies, it does retain direct control over a number of agencies that perform functions for the legislature. This control is usually exercised by either legislative members serving on the governing boards or through legislative appointments to the boards. Among these agencies are the Legislative Audit Council, which performs audits of state programs and agencies upon the request of legislators. The General Assembly also selects the members of the Public Service Commission, which exercises quasi-legislative functions in approving the rates of private water, electricity, and sewer utilities. And the legislature controls the Agency Salary Head Commission, which approves salaries of the leaders of various state agencies, including universities.

The General Assembly also controls the Joint Bond Review Committee, which must be consulted on various indebtednesses and capital expenditures of state government and agencies. This committee has emerged as a seat of power in state government. While not officially given the authority to "approve" proposals, a "recommendation not to approve" effectively equates to a death sentence for any such proposal.

The General Assembly shares control of several important state agencies whose functions intersect the executive and legislative branches. Again this control is exercised by either legislative members serving on the governing boards or through appointment power to the boards. These governing boards usually have appointments from both the legislative bodies and the executive branch. Included in these agencies are the State Fiscal Affairs Agency and the Board of Economic Advisors, which consider certain financial matters for the state, colleges, and universities; the Education Oversight Committee; the State Infrastructure Bank; and the First Steps Board. Important state agencies and their governance structures will be discussed in chapter 5.

Since its inception South Carolina hewed to the principle that the legislature was the people's branch of government and should be the dominant force of government. Over time the state has seen a true separation of powers develop. Notable in the modern era is the dramatic strengthening of the governor's office, discussed in the next chapter. However, through it all South Carolina's General Assembly remains an extremely powerful force in the state.

3

The Executive Branch

The Governor, a Growing Power

In this section we will discuss the historical growth of the governor's office from a two-year position appointed by the General Assembly to a four-year position elected by the public with very limited powers and finally to a two-term position with real powers of agency appointment; a robust staff; budgetary influence; and a strong, public bully pulpit. National comparisons of the strength of the executive branch in a state in relation to its legislature are notably difficult to make due to the unique structure of each state government, the informal powers that accrue from state to state, and the somewhat arbitrary nature of any criteria used to measure power and effectiveness.[1] However over the last fifty years South Carolina has seen a tremendous strengthening of the governor's office, often with power shifting away from the legislature, which has brought the state closer to the norm of other states' power structures. South Carolina's strengthening of the governor's office is in notable contrast to North Carolina, which over the last decade has stripped gubernatorial powers and reasserted legislative controls tinged with a partisan color.[2]

South Carolina has elected its fair share of colorful governors. In times of turmoil and change governors seem to accrue more power and influence demonstrated by the ascension of Wade Hampton during the reconstruction era and the active leadership of governors in the modern era such as Fritz Hollings, Bob McNair, John West, and Carroll Campbell.

Two of the most important figures to occupy the governor's office were "Pitchfork" Ben Tillman and Richard "Dick" Riley. The men served in contrastingly different times and had vastly different beliefs in and approaches to government. But each man revealed that very real power lay dormant in the governor's office waiting to be unleashed by the right occupants. Their lives and their tenures in office elucidate the power that is inherent in the central executive branch office when occupied by forceful and committed personalities and the growth of the office over time. For good in one instance and bad in the other, these two governors arguably had more impact on South Carolina than any other executives.

Benjamin R. Tillman and the Brutality of Power

Benjamin R. Tillman was born in 1847 and lived until 1918, spanning the antebellum era, the Civil War, Reconstruction, White conservative retrenchment, and the Jim Crow era.[3] Tillman was an economic populist and a racial reactionary; his influence on South Carolina would be dramatic and lasting. He captured the state's Democratic Party when it was a Whites-only club and used it to enact a populist economic agenda and reactionary, racist restrictions.

Tillman grew up in rural Edgefield County, working on a successful farm on which his family owned land and enslaved approximately one hundred people. A serious illness in childhood resulted in the loss of his left eye and kept him out of the Civil War. Tillman and his family managed to hold onto their land after the war. But in 1881, Tillman's farm was caught in a series of droughts and crop failures that set back his economic fortunes. He began to engage vigorously in public affairs, advocating for agricultural education and diversification, helping to found the Edgefield Agricultural Society, and participating in the farmers' movement of the era. Tillman quickly became known for acerbic and powerful speeches attacking Black citizens and the conservative Bourbon White leadership in the state. He talked of "lazy negroes" and "demagogues and lawyers in the pay of finance."[4] He presented himself as a champion of the rural farmers against lawyers, politicians, merchants, and aristocrats. He was a master of the sound bite and emotional politics.

FIGURE 3. *Benjamin Tillman, ca. 1918. Library of Congress Prints and Photographs Division, LC-USZ62-34404.*

As he became more politically active he viciously attacked the Conservative White establishment and bragged about his violent action against South Carolina's Black citizens. In short, he mastered the art of political demagoguery.

By 1890, Tillman's influence dominated the Democratic Party's membership, ensuring his nomination for governor at the party's convention. His politics were so extreme that a contingent of establishment Conservative members bolted the party and nominated a candidate for the general election, seeking to rally Black voters still eligible to vote and more conservative White voters. The effort was in vain. Tillman was elected governor in a landslide election, losing only Beaufort and Berkley Counties, both of which had large Black voting populations. In the election Tillman's support came not only from the rural White farmers but from White voters across South

Carolina, who were wedded to the Democratic Party's fundamental purpose of keeping Black citizens from power.

As governor Tillman was ruthlessly effective. He and his allies in the General Assembly swept away the remnants of Black participation in government and of White Conservative leadership. Former Confederate General, former Governor, and then-Senator Wade Hampton was humiliatingly defeated in his bid for reelection to the United States Senate by Tillman's supporters in the General Assembly. In his inaugural address Tillman stated that "the Whites have absolute control of the State government, and we intend at any and all hazards to retain it."[5] He attacked the University of South Carolina as an embodiment of the state's elites and supported the creation and growth of Clemson and Winthrop as counterforces for educating the common White citizen.

Tillman was renominated for a second two-year term by the Democratic Party over opposition from the traditional Conservatives such as Hampton. And Tillmanites dominated the makeup of the state's House of Representatives and Senate ensuring enactments that favored the White population and the diminishment of Blacks' rights. Tillman effectively used his position as governor to advocate for his dream of a White-dominated, populist state and elected his acolytes to all positions of power.

As his final term as governor wound down Tillman set his sights on the United States Senate and declared that he would go "to Washington with a pitchfork, and prod him [President Grover Cleveland] in his old fat ribs."[6] In the US Senate Tillman continued his hostile and repugnant characterizations of Black people and fought any efforts to empower Black South Carolinians. Tillman's most consequential efforts came in 1895, when he orchestrated the state constitutional convention of that year, formally stripping Black participation in voting and government while also diluting local governments from exercising power. Tillman showed how ruthlessly an effective person could use the governor's office to achieve his ends.

FIGURE 4. *Governor Richard Riley signs a document to observe Library Week, ca. 1983. Copyright © Richland Library. All rights reserved. For more information, contact the Walker Local and Family History Center at Richland Library, Columbia, SC 29201.*

Richard "Dick" Riley, Leading a Changing South Carolina

Eighty-one years after Tillman left the governor's office a remarkably different man in a remarkably different Democratic Party was elected to fill that position.[7] Richard "Dick" Riley was born in 1933, just fifteen years after the death of Ben Tillman. During Riley's political career South Carolina would be transformed from a rural, impoverished, explicitly racist society into a modern economic powerhouse with civil rights protections. And the Democratic Party he belonged to would shed its Whites-only label and become a political home for most Black voters, while White voters increasingly embraced the Republican Party.

Riley's political life coincided with a rare progressive era in South Carolina's politics and government, and he made the most of this opportunity. But first he had to face personal adversity. Riley served in the United States Navy from 1954 until 1956, and while there he was diagnosed with spondylitis. An extremely painful bone disease affecting the spine, it quickly caused Riley's back to curve forward, locking his neck in place, unable to turn from side to side. But this normally debilitating disease did not stop Dick Riley from pursuing his dreams.

After his service in the navy, Riley was accepted to the University of South Carolina School of Law and eventually joined his father's law firm in Greenville. Like so many of the state's major political figures, Riley was first elected to the state House of Representatives in 1962 from his home county of Greenville, and four years later he was elected to the state Senate. Riley quickly joined other progressively minded legislators, and together they were dubbed the "Young Turks."[8] These young Democratic legislators led efforts to modernize the state's government, improve the education system, and desegregate the racially divided legal and cultural system that dominated the state.

In 1978, Riley defeated better-known candidates to win the Democratic gubernatorial primary and went on to win the general election with over 60 percent of the vote. As governor Riley led an ambitious effort to improve utility regulation, block nuclear waste dumping, aid the medically indigent, and change the state constitution to allow governors to serve two four-year terms. Riley would go on to be the first person ever elected in South Carolina to two four-year terms as governor when he was reelected with over 70 percent of the vote.

In his second term Riley made education reform and improvement, the touchstone of his efforts. With a massive statewide mobilization of citizens Riley persuaded the legislature to increase the sales tax to provide school funding, extend the school day, and provide increased pay for teachers. His efforts were admired nationwide, and after leaving office Riley was selected by President Bill Clinton to serve as the United States Secretary of Education. Upon retirement from the federal government Riley was hailed as "one of the great statesmen of education."[9] Throughout his political career his kindness, humility, and respect toward others shone as an effective counterexample to the likes of Ben Tillman and the Tillmanites who once ruled South Carolina.

History of the Governorship

From the end of British rule until the mid-twentieth century, governors played a mostly symbolic role in South Carolina. Terms were short, powers limited, executive authority divided, and executive appointments controlled by the General Assembly. But beginning in the 1950s, the State saw an increasing number of high-profile governors aggregate more and more informal power, eventually leading to pushes for formal, structural reordering of power that favored the governor's office. Strom Thurmond, Fritz Hollings, Bob McNair, Dick Riley, and Carroll Campbell were popular figures in the state who successfully rallied business elites, the media, and political party structures to support increased power being given to the governor's office, generally at the expense of the General Assembly.

South Carolina's distrust of strong executive figures came honestly. In 1670, the Lords Proprietors appointed William Sayle, the first governor of the Carolinas in Charleston.[10] Twenty-six governors served the colony of South Carolina under British rule, ending with the American Revolution.[11] Their governance and rule helped sow the original and long-standing distrust of centralized authority in South Carolina that lasted for generations. The American Revolution caused the evacuation of the royal governor. Under state rule, the governorship was purposely reduced to a highly symbolic and powerless office selected by the General Assembly and serving for a two-year term. Governors had no veto power. The position was treated as a political figurehead and as an honor granted by the General Assembly for good service to the state. This simple "symbolic governor" lasted until the Civil War.

At the conclusion of the war, the victorious United States government appointed a governor for South Carolina until such time as a new constitution was adopted giving free Blacks the right to vote. Initially the Constitutional Convention of 1865 recognized that slavery was abolished but did little else to empower Black citizens. In fact the 1865 constitution was an attempt by the antebellum White power structure to reestablish its control by enacting the "Black Codes" restricting the rights of Blacks to engage in commerce, prohibiting for the first time interracial marriages, and defining when a person was considered Black or White.[12] That constitution also had effects on the evolution of the state's government structure. For the first time a South Carolina constitution provided for the popular election of its governor, gave governors a veto power, created new districts for legislators from which to be elected, and took away the property ownership requirement for voting.[13] Like its predecessors this constitution was not submitted to voters for approval.

The national goal of allowing freed Black people in the South the right to vote was not easy in coming. In 1868, under new federal leadership and an occupying army a state constitutional convention convened that included 124 persons, 73 of whom were Black and 51 of whom were White.[14] Over the next few years South Carolina would elect the nation's first Black person to be seated in Congress, appoint a Black state Supreme Court justice, and have numerous Black elected officials. Congressman Robert Smalls and Justice Jonathon Jasper Wright were among the groundbreaking luminaries of this era. Meanwhile Whites would maintain a prolonged insurgency effort through violence, economics, and politics in an effort to overthrow Black political participation and equal rights.[15]

The progressive Constitution of 1868[16] guaranteed the right to vote of all twenty-one--year-old male citizens regardless of race. It also continued the 1865 change, making the governorship popularly elected to a four-year term. This seemingly small yet radical change in government structure was a first step toward an independent governor's office that a hundred years later would act as a true separate and coequal branch of government. The governor was given a veto power; command of the state militia; pardon authority; and other meaningful, if limited, functions. Although South Carolina's Reconstruction government gave the governor's office new relevance, it maintained the entrenched power of the "legislative state." During this brief period when African Americans exercised substantial government power, South Carolina maintained its historic model of diffused government power predominated by the "people's branch."

In the 1890s rural populist Whites led a vicious backlash against any and all political and economic gains by Black citizens in South Carolina. The so-called Reform movement overturned both the re-emerging antebellum White Bourbon leadership, embodied in the person of Wade Hampton, and snuffed out any hopes of Black political participation with the rise to power of Benjamin "Pitchfork" Tillman. Tillman emerged as the clear leader in the effort to empower poor, rural Whites while oppressing the Black population. He was elected governor in 1890. At his inaugural address, Pitchfork Ben did not disappoint the populist throngs who gathered to watch him sworn into office. "'The whites,' he thundered, 'have absolute control of the State government, and we intend any and all hazards to retain it.'"[17]

This White Reformer domination continued the rollback of Black political and civic power that had begun under the Conservative restoration, which would last for generations. It also changed the governmental structure of South Carolina, creating a new constitution in 1895 that enshrined the diminution of Black political power. The constitution, however, also created a delineation between legislative and executive branch power with the beginnings of a system of checks and balances, although that delineation remained fuzzy.[18] Once again, legislative dominance remained, with many state agency appointments controlled by the General Assembly, executive power diffused among numerous elected statewide officials, and governors' terms being only two years with the potential for only one reelection.[19]

The 1895 constitution remains the constitution of South Carolina, although it has been amended many times. Under the state constitution, the governor is considered the "chief magistrate." Governors must be at least thirty years old, must not deny the existence of a Supreme Being, and must be citizens of the United States and residents of South Carolina for at least five years. The United States Supreme Court's interpretation of the US Constitution has nullified the requirement of belief in a higher being, but the other qualifications remain in effect. Governors are also the "commander in chief" of the organized and unorganized militias within the state. In 1927, governors' terms were set for a single four-year period, and by constitutional amendment governors became able to serve two four-year terms starting in 1982, as discussed above. The elections are held in even-numbered years, which is different from those of the state Senate. Unlike in some states, governors in South Carolina do not have the power to issues pardons, although they may commute death sentences.

In the latter part of the 1950s a renaissance in the push for executive power had a momentous effect on governmental power structure in South Carolina. Governors such as James Byrnes and Fritz Hollings in the 1950s and Robert McNair and John Carl West in the 1960s and 1970s played high-profile roles within the state government and pushed for major legislative and executive initiatives. This increased activity by the governors and push for more formal powers was marked by initial incremental progress, culminating in a period of rapid aggregation of power from 1980 to the present. Under the leadership of Governor Richard "Dick" Riley and supportive legislators, governors were allowed to run for a second four-year term beginning in 1982.

The Government Restructuring Act of 1994, enacted with the strong support of Governor Carroll Campbell and Speaker Robert J. Sheheen (this author's uncle), created a cabinet for the governor with many major agency heads appointed directly by the governor's office. Over time, the governor's office became the appointing authority of almost every executive agency—from cabinet directors to state boards and other executive governmental agencies in South Carolina. With the traditional advice and consent of the state Senate, the governor now appoints all cabinet agencies, the board of the Department of Transportation, the board of the Department of Natural Resources, and many other major agency leaders.

Furthermore the number of statewide elected officials has been reduced, coming more in line with the average of other states. Governors now select their own lieutenant governor and appoint the state's military leader, the adjutant general. With the creation of the Department of Administration in the Restructuring Act of 2014, the governor was given real powers over governmental administrative functions. The act also empowered and formalized the Executive Budget Office, increasing a governor's ability to influence the traditionally legislative function of budgeting and appropriating for state government.

The governor of South Carolina is now the single most important governmental figure in the state. Coupled with the informal power of the bully pulpit and popular support used by effective governors, the position directly controls or influences all functions of state government. The governorship has long surpassed its meager origins and consolidated great formal, structural, and informal power in its office.

Structure and Powers of the Governor's Office

Governors exercise formal power through the line-item veto, appointments to agency leadership, budgetary proposals, and many other direct tools. Effective governors also exercise great informal power through the shaping of public opinion and the relationships the governor builds with legislators, agency leaders, business executives, local officials, and other influential persons.

Governor's Staff

Governors have great flexibility in the organization of their staff.[20] However they rely on the General Assembly to fund the positions they find necessary. Out of respect for the separation of powers the General Assembly has historically acceded to the wishes of governors for office funding and staff.

Governors typically organize their immediate staff with a chief of staff at the top of the office hierarchy. Chiefs of staff often hold considerable clout. They may act as "gatekeepers," parceling out access to a governor, and they are perceived as speaking for the governor when they meet with others. Furthermore chiefs of staff often make internal policy decisions that affect the operations of state government. Several policy advisers, legislative liaisons, press secretaries, and legal counsels round out the office staff. Governors' office staff number about a dozen people. However a governor has almost the entire executive branch to call upon for expertise and assistance as needed. For example, governors have security personnel, drivers, and aides provided by the State Law Enforcement Division and the State Protective Services, and governors regularly meet with agency heads for advice, updates, and information. If a governor asks for support from a state agency, it will be provided.

The Veto

Under Article IV, Section 21 of South Carolina's constitution, every bill must be presented to the governor for consideration. Within five days, excluding Sunday, the governor may veto the bill, sign the bill, or fail to take action. If the governor fails to take action, the bill becomes a law without the governor's signature. If the governor vetoes the bill, the legislature may override with two-thirds support of both bodies, and the bill becomes law.

The so-called line-item veto can be an extremely effective tool for governors to use; it is a power most US presidents would covet. The South Carolina governor's line-item veto reflects a power common to governors across the United States.[21] The line-item veto is only available for bills appropriating moneys from the state treasury. This power allows a governor to dig deeply into specific and discrete portions of budget bills, vetoing any unwanted appropriations or policy changes contained within them. A governor may delete "distinct items and sections" from such bills, cut spending overall, or substantially change the state's budgetary priorities. This gubernatorial power is not without limitations. For example many states allow a governor to not simply delete distinct items, but also to reduce appropriations by whatever amount a governor wishes. South Carolina's traditional respect for legislative dominance on budgetary matters means such a controlling veto power is not given to the governor's office.

Historically the General Assembly has jealously guarded its constitutional powers to determine appropriations of state funds, and it has frequently overridden governors' line-item vetoes. Furthermore governors are not allowed to veto language within a budget bill changing the specific intent of the General Assembly. For example, South Carolina's state supreme court has established that a governor may not change the words "shall not" to "shall" by deleting the word "not." Even with the restrictions placed on the line-item veto, it is an incredibly powerful tool to change or draw attention to the spending priorities of the state and shape the debate and outcome of how funds are allocated. A governor now has real budgetary influence in South Carolina.

Agency Appointments

As mentioned previously the General Assembly dominated the appointment and control of state commissions and agencies for most of South Carolina's history. This model was in large part based on the corrupting influence that a concentration of power in one person has on government. But in the modern era of complex society and correspondingly complicated government structures, the General Assembly has gradually ceded most of the executive appointment power to the governor's office in hopes of better efficiency and accountability. Currently, the governor appoints almost all the directors or commissioners of state government's major agencies.

Notably the Department of Administration was created under the Restructuring Act of 2014, consolidating the administrative functions of state government under the governors' appointee, including those of vehicle and property management, human resources, and technology management. Such functions formerly were managed by an agency called the Budget and Control Board, which was controlled by members of both the executive and legislative branches. The Department of Administration also subsumed miscellaneous functions formerly housed in the governor's office, such as the Office of Veterans Affairs and the Guardian Ad Litem Program; the latter advocates for abused and neglected children.

Most of the critically important state agencies now have their agency directors appointed directly by the governor with the advice and consent of the Senate. Advocates of this direct appointment model argue that direct gubernatorial appointment of agency directors should make those agencies more accountable to the governor and therefore to the citizens. Agencies with the direct appointment model include

- Department of Administration
- Department of Alcohol and Other Drug Abuse
- Department of Commerce
- Department of Consumer Affairs
- Department of Corrections
- Department of Environmental Services
- Department of Health and Human Services
- Department of Insurance
- Department of Juvenile Justice
- Department of Labor, Licensing, and Regulation
- Department of Motor Vehicles
- Department of Parks, Recreation, and Tourism
- Department of Probation, Pardon, and Parole
- Department of Public Safety
- Department of Revenue
- Department of Social Services
- Employment Security Commission
- State Law Enforcement Division

Most other major state agencies are also controlled by gubernatorial appointment, but through the commission model. Under the commission model the governor appoints the governing boards or commissions of the agencies, and the boards hire the executive directors and make major policy decisions for the agency. Under this model the governor's appointments are also usually subject to advice and consent of the Senate. Advocates for this model argue that it creates more transparency in decision-making and stability in operations, allows for a more professional career civil service, and buffers state agencies from the whims of governors' political calculations while still allowing governors to set the broad policy positions of agencies through board appointments. Among the major agencies established under this model are

- Forestry Commission
- Department of Public Health
- State Housing Authority
- Department of Mental Health

- Department of Natural Resources
- Department of Transportation
- Department of Vocational Rehabilitation

In addition to appointing the leadership of major state agencies, a governor will have the opportunity to fill over fifteen hundred appointments, many of them to unpaid civic commissions. These commissions cover hundreds of topic areas and include such entities as the Children's Trust Fund and the Sestercentennial Commission. The governor also appoints ceremonial positions such as the state's poet laureate. Recent governors have often failed to fully embrace their appointment powers and left scores of these politically more minor, yet substantively important, positions unappointed.

Governors also make many regional or local government appointments. While usually deferring to the nominations of local legislators, governors appoint officials such as county magistrates, local election commissioners, members of the regional Foster Care Review Boards, and members of water and sewer authorities.

Executive Budget Powers

As in most other states and our federal government, the constitution of South Carolina vests the primary power of financial appropriations and budgets with the legislative branch. Historically governors played little role in the decision on how to tax or spend moneys within the state. However under the Restructuring Act of 1994 the governor received the power to submit an executive budget to the General Assembly within five days of the legislature assembling. Over time this process has allowed governors to "set the table" for agency expenditures. Even after 1994, governors remained hobbled in impacting expenditures because of their small staffs and lack of budgetary expertise within their offices.

A governor's ability to influence the budget process was further strengthened in the Restructuring Act of 2014. In that act, the governor was vested with independent staff and expertise by creating the Executive Budget Office. The Executive Budget Office is housed in the Department of Administration and is responsible for developing the governor's budget proposal. It also provides oversight of the annual state budget. The agency oversees annual accountability reports for state agencies and has oversight of permanent improvement projects.

Beginning in the fall of a given year a governor's office typically requires state agencies to submit budget requests. These requests are then considered and evaluated in the creation of an executive budget. An executive budget has no legal effect, but it does affect the ultimate legislative budget by shaping agency requests and giving an imprimatur of legitimacy to those requests. In recent years governors have effectively used this process to control agency requests for funding. Frequently legislators hear agency directors behind closed doors complain that the true funding needs of the agency were being quashed by the governor's office through the executive budget process. Nevertheless governors have become quite effective at shaping the budgets for the executive agencies.

A governor's budget proposal for state agencies is often followed by the General Assembly. However governors' budget proposals for non–executive branch expenditures are not persuasive. Governors' recommendations relating to major infrastructure projects, higher education funding, and other non-executive agency operations are frequently ignored by the General Assembly.

Informal Powers

Effective governors can marshal more informal power than any other officeholder in South Carolina. Such power stems from two main sources. First, the governor is the only state-level elected official who is well known by a majority of voters within the State. Governors' campaigns are high profile, expensive, and result in many interactions with citizens, both personally and through paid and unpaid media. Once they take office governors can communicate with citizens through the apparatus of government and through the attention paid by media sources. Citizens often identify with the governor as the embodiment of the state. This connection allows an effective governor, and only the governor, to rally segments of the population to support a broad range of issues, legislation, or causes.

Effective governors also use formal powers to create informal power through other leaders. Governors invite legislators to the Governor's Mansion to woo support on gubernatorial priorities.

Governors make appointments as rewards to political, business, and civic leaders who then help accomplish goals. Governors support causes favored by important constituencies to then receive support from those constituencies for the governor's agenda.

A governor's ability to create, aggregate, and capitalize informal power is limited only by imagination and a will to work.

Miscellaneous Powers

Governors in South Carolina are vested with many miscellaneous powers that are often overlooked but which contain the potential for great influence. Among these are the power to declare a state of emergency and take extraordinary control over law enforcement and the State Guard. By statute governors are allowed to suspend, and in certain circumstances remove, certain local and state elected and appointed officials who are charged with crimes or are guilty of malfeasance, misfeasance, incompetency, absenteeism, conflicts of interests, misconduct, persistent neglect of duty, or incapacity. Governors are empowered to name interim replacements for such officials.

Governors also have the power to call the legislature back into session when "extraordinary occasions" arise. However due to abuses by some recent governors the legislature rarely officially adjourns for the year but instead simply "recedes" from meeting. It thus thwarts an overbearing governor from using the extraordinary session power to dictate meetings of the General Assembly.

Due to abuses in the early 1900s, governors in South Carolina no longer hold the power to pardon crimes. However they do have the ability to grant clemency in death penalty cases.

Governors in South Carolina are required by law to reside in the capital city of Columbia. They exercise control over the Governor's Mansion compound, which consists of the governor's residence and the historic homes located there: the Lace House, the Caldwell-Boylston House, and their associated gardens.

Brief Comparisons

Various attempts have been made to categorize and compare governors' powers across the United States. Notable scholars include Joseph Schlesinger and Thad Beyle in the 1960s, who issued comparison updates through the decades. Historically South Carolina's governors ranked low in formal powers compared to other states, with the last of Beyle's updates having been carried out more than a decade ago. These formulas have been criticized as looking at a limited menu of powers, being unable to account for the variety of state government structures, and changing the criteria for evaluation over time.[22]

One category of a governor's informal power that is often overlooked is the unitary partisan makeup of the legislature and the governor's office.[23] South Carolina has historically been a one-party state with the same party controlling the legislature and the governor's office. This partisan, unitary control can be a strong source of political power for a governor as governors are seen as the leader of their political parties within a state and thus have political influence over other elected members of their party, including legislators.

Significant formal power granted to the governor's office over the last several decades, coupled with the occupant's statewide stature and partisan leadership, have created a truly powerful political position. Although having arisen from a mostly ceremonial origin, governors in South Carolina now wield tremendous formal and informal power.

Other Executive Branch Officials

South Carolina has numerous other officeholders who are generally considered members of the executive branch. Some of these officeholders, such as the superintendent of education, are created by the state's constitution and are discussed below. Many other important executive-branch positions and agencies are created by statute and are discussed in chapter 5.

Attorney General (the State's Lawyer)

The attorney general is an ancient and powerful position in South Carolina. Appointed by the Lords Proprietors in 1698 and arriving in the colony in 1699, Nicholas Trott was the first attorney general of South Carolina.[24] Like so many other early South Carolinians, Trott's family was involved in trade in the Caribbean islands, and Trott had previously served as attorney general of Bermuda.

Although the powers of the attorney general are those of an executive-branch official, in South Carolina's constitution the office's powers are set forth in the section empowering the Judicial Department. This arrangement has likely occurred because an understanding of the independent nature of the judiciary and the separation of powers developed slowly in the United States and even more so in South Carolina. Article V of the South Carolina constitution holds that "the Attorney General shall be the chief prosecuting officer of the State with authority to supervise the prosecution of all criminal cases in courts of record." South Carolina courts have described the authority of the attorney general as including "all such power and authority as public interests may, from time to time, require, and may institute, conduct and maintain all such suits and proceedings as he deems necessary for the enforcement of the laws of the State, the preservation of order, and the protection of public rights."[25] The office of the attorney general derives its authority from the state constitution, court-created common law, and legislative enactments.

Like much of South Carolina government, the General Assembly historically exercised great control over the position of attorney general. Following the American Revolution, the General Assembly continued the preexisting office and took on the power of selecting its holder. During the latter part of the 1800s, the position became popularly elected with a term of two years, eventually transitioning to four-year terms. No term limits apply to the office of the attorney general, allowing occupants to build experience, knowledge, relationships, and power over time.

For much of its history, the attorney general's office was staffed by only a secretary and then a few lawyers. But with the development of a large, complex society and a complicated economy, the office has grown into approximately ninety attorneys with staff support of an additional two hundred people, including investigators, paralegals, and subject-matter specialists. Broadly speaking the attorney general's powers reflect the divisions made within the state's court system between civil authority and criminal authority.

Under constitutional authority as chief prosecuting officer, the attorney general

- holds supervisory authority over the prosecution of all criminal cases, which are generally handled by locally elected solicitors;
- oversees the investigative and prosecution activities of the state grand jury including multijurisdictional drug offenders, obscenity cases, public corruption, election fraud, computer crime violations, terrorism, and securities fraud;
- represents the state in all appeals of criminal convictions;
- represents the state in all death penalty appeals in both state and federal courts after conviction;
- investigates and prosecutes cases of internet crimes against children, including those involving sexual exploitation;
- investigates and prosecutes cases of Medicaid provider and recipient fraud, and the abuse, neglect, and exploitation of vulnerable adults;
- represents the state in civil confinement trials of alleged sexually violent predators under South Carolina's Sexually Violent Predators statute;
- supervises and prosecutes cases of insurance fraud;
- prosecutes violations of state tax laws;
- assists victims of crimes in claiming the benefits guaranteed under the state's Victims Bill of Rights; and
- represents the state when convicted defendants file for post-conviction relief in state trial and appellate courts.

Under the common law and statutory authority as chief legal officer, the attorney general

- represents and advises the state, its agencies, political subdivision, and officials in legal matters when the state is a party to a legal action;
- is responsible for employing and supervising attorneys who represent the state, as well as overseeing the state's litigation and effectuating South Carolina's legal policy;
- issues official legal opinions upon request by constitutional officers, members of the General Assembly, and certain state and local officials; and

- acts as securities commissioner, overseeing the registration of sellers of securities, investigating fraud and violations of securities laws, and providing information on securities laws and practices.

Much like a governor, effective attorneys general also accrue and exercise informal power. Attorneys general frequently communicate and build relationships with legislators to influence the passing or repealing of laws relating to the office or to the criminal code. Furthermore attorneys general, with the help of like-minded legislators, are often able to block the passage of laws that they do not support.

Successful attorneys general are also able to build up important support among specific constituencies such as law enforcement, victims' rights groups, and other groups with an interest in criminal or civil law. These groups often rally to support initiatives that an attorney general may promote. Finally, the attorney general is perhaps the only executive branch official, besides a governor, who can command some broad level of media attention for wide-ranging actions and goals of the office.

Superintendent of Education, a Gift from Reconstruction

The position of superintendent of education grew out of the Reconstruction era and the resulting empowerment of Black officials coupled with support from White Republican officeholders. The Constitution of 1868 laid out, for the first time in South Carolina, the principles of a free public education, taxation for schools, higher education, and other universal educational opportunities. The 1868 Constitution held that "the supervision of public instruction shall be vested in a State Superintendent of Education, who shall be elected by qualified electors." The separate election of a superintendent continues to this day, with voters overwhelmingly rejecting in 2018 an effort to make it an appointed position.[26] The 1868 Constitution further required that "the General Assembly shall [. . .] provide for a liberal and uniform system of free public schools throughout the state and shall also make provision for the division of the State into suitable School Districts." The Department of Education was established shortly thereafter by legislative enactment.

Although the superintendent of education is the highest profile and most powerful education leader in the state, South Carolina's education system has many layers of governance. The State Board of Education, selected by the legislature, creates and adopts general policies and procedures for schools to follow. The state superintendent is tasked with implementing and enforcing those policies. Local school districts are governed by local school boards and managed by local school superintendents. However in certain instances the state superintendent has the authority and power to temporarily "take over" local districts that are in crisis, making policy decisions and managing the district.

In the role as leader of the State Department of Education, the superintendent also provides professional, technological, and financial support and training for districts. The office is involved in approving textbooks that may be used in the state. Uniquely, the superintendent's office, through the Department of Education, operates and manages the entire school bus fleet for the state of South Carolina. In other states, buses are owned and managed by local districts or local governments.

Successful superintendents' informal power perhaps equals or exceeds the formal powers of the office. As the only statewide elected official tasked with promoting education, effective superintendents are often able to marshal teachers, parents, and the media on issues relating to education. The General Assembly has dedicated the largest portion of state funds to education in every budget in the modern era, and a respected superintendent's initiatives, recommendations, and requests carry great weight in shaping these investments.

Treasurer: The Banker

Article VI, Section 7 of the South Carolina Constitution establishes the office of the treasurer to be elected by the voters for four-year terms. The duties and powers of the treasurer are created by statutes passed by the General Assembly. The bulk of that authority and responsibility is set forth in Title 11, Chapter 5 of the South Carolina code.

The office of the state treasurer has a long history, having been created for the first time during the colonial era. Colonial treasurers often commingled personal and public funds in their safekeeping, a practice that was not necessarily deemed corrupt at the time.[27] However this commingling led to several treasurers owing massive debts to the public. Corruption in the treasurer's office perhaps reached its pinnacle during the Reconstruction years. Although many progressive accomplishments occurred during this period in South Carolina, the chaos that was often present resulted in flagrant corruption by some individuals. State Treasurer Niles Parker helped lead a scheme that diverted huge sums of state bond proceeds for private gain. He was eventually prosecuted and convicted.[28] These types of abuses led to the creation of the Comptroller General's Office in 1890 as we know it today, which acts as a check and complement to the operations of the Office of the State Treasurer.

In a way the Office of the State Treasurer serves as the banker for South Carolina's state government. It is responsible for the safety and security of the state's money, investments, and debts. Among the duties of the treasurer is the submission of an annual financial report to the General Assembly. The treasurer also acts as an independent voice providing financial information and perspective for the part-time General Assembly and the public, separate from that of the governor's office.

The Office of the State Treasurer has organized itself into a variety of divisions:

- The Banking and Investment Management Division manages specialized banking services for state agencies and universities. It also performs daily cash-management functions to maximize investment opportunities for the state. The staff invests and manages state and local government funds with the goals of preserving capital, maintaining liquidity, and obtaining the best return within the appropriate risk measurements.
- The Debt Management Division is responsible for managing the debt for the state, optimizing the debt structure and ensuring timely repayment of debt.
- The Programs Division oversees various financial programs created by state law, including the Future Scholar 529

College Savings Plan, the SC Tuition Prepayment Program, the Palmetto ABLE Savings Program, and the state's Unclaimed Property Program.
- The Treasury Management Division is responsible for the daily accounting of all cash disbursement and depository activities of the state. It also administers all court fees and fines collected throughout the state. The treasurer also manages the state's Aid to Subdivisions program, which provides direct funding from the state to local governments.

Comptroller General: The Accountant

This little-understood office is often overlooked as part of South Carolina's state government system. If the state treasurer can be thought of as the state's banker, the comptroller can be thought of as the state's accountant. Although some officials had previously been designated as a comptroller general during the early years of the state's history, the office as we know it today was created in 1890 in response to corrupt practices by the state treasurer and other officials during the Reconstruction era. The Office of the Comptroller General is authorized under Title VI, Section 7 of the South Carolina Constitution and is elected by voters of the state to four-year terms of office. Its duties are laid out in Article XI, Section 3 of the South Carolina Code of Laws.

The comptroller general's most important task is to examine every payment proposed by state government agencies and officials to ensure the payments are properly authorized, that funds are available to cover them, and that they are properly classified in the state's accounting system. If the expenditures are deemed proper then the comptroller general issues warrants authorizing the treasurer to make payment of the funds out of the state treasury. The comptroller general also inspects payments made by the treasurer to ensure they were made in conformity with the authorized warrants. This system of double checks is designed to avert improper, fraudulent, or corrupt expenditures.

The comptroller general also maintains the state's accounting system, establishes internal controls for state agencies, provides financial services to agencies and local governments, and prepares reports on financial operations and conditions of state government.

Secretary of State: Pencil and Paper and Databases

The secretary of state's office can trace its roots to South Carolina's period of colonial governance under the Lords Proprietors. As population grew and government became more formalized, a need for record keeping and preservation arose. The secretary of state's position was established to fill this need. Following the Declaration of Independence, the South Carolina Constitution of 1776 enshrined the office of secretary of state. Following the concept of popular, legislative dominance, the General Assembly was entrusted with electing the secretary. For most of the antebellum period the office remained tasked with its original purpose of record keeping and preservation. The post–Civil War period saw greater empowerment of the office, including handling the incorporation of new towns, countersigning many gubernatorial appointments, and certifying the elections of state officials. It is important to note that the office also became popularly elected.

In the twentieth century, an additional hodgepodge of areas was assigned to the secretary of state's office through legislation. These responsibilities include the registering of corporate entities, commissioning of notaries, monitoring nonprofit corporations' legal compliance, administering of charitable laws, recording and regulating Uniform Commercial Code transactions, and monitoring government-appointed boards and commissions. Much debate in the modern era has occurred around whether the secretary of state should remain an independently elected office, become one appointed by the governor, or simply be consolidated into another agency.

Agriculture Commissioner: From Farm to City

South Carolina is one of only twelve states that elects its agriculture commissioner. The South Carolina Department of Agriculture was established in 1879 to oversee and promote agriculture. Its creation followed a wave of agricultural political activism by small farmers and farmers' movements across the United States. Current services include food safety inspections, gas pump inspections, entrepreneurship development, and the Certified South Carolina branding program.

Lieutenant Governor: Worth the Salary?

Like the governor's office, that of the lieutenant governor dates back to the colonial period of South Carolina. Since that time the core purpose of the office has simply been to succeed the governor if the governor is no longer able to serve due to death, infirmity, impeachment, or other reason. After the Revolutionary War, the General Assembly selected who the lieutenant governor would be. The office became popularly elected following the Civil War and ran separately from that of the governor until the early twenty-first century. Thus at periods in the state's history, the governor and lieutenant governor belonged to different political parties, reflecting the swing voting pattern that existed for only a very brief period in the state.[29]

For most of its history the lieutenant governor presided over the South Carolina Senate, giving its holder a high profile within the workings of state government. However voters approved a constitutional amendment that removed the lieutenant governor from the state Senate chamber while also making the office one selected by the governor instead of being popularly elected, beginning in 2018. This change seems to have had the interesting effect of making a little-known and inconsequential position even less well known and less consequential. The office of lieutenant governor now has little visibility or structural power in South Carolina. Its occupants are entirely dependent on the governor's office for any responsibilities or allocation of duties.

Adjutant General: The State's Military

The adjutant general is head of the South Carolina Military Department, administering the affairs of the Army and Air National Guard, the Emergency Management Division, the State Guard, and the Youth Challenge Academy. The governor is by law the Commander in Chief, with the adjutant general holding the rank of major general. The adjutant general's office has existed since shortly after the American Declaration of Independence. In keeping with the philosophy of a powerful, popularly controlled legislature, the General

Assembly selected its occupants until the Constitution of 1868. At that time the office became popularly elected. During the twentieth century it remained the only popularly elected adjutant general's office in the United States. However, a constitutional amendment approved by voters gave the selection of this office to the governor beginning in 2019.

Most notable in South Carolina's executive branch is the increased power granted to and exercised in the governor's office. From humble beginnings of a two-year position selected by the General Assembly, the governor now wields tremendous powers and is far and away the most recognizable state official.

4

The Judicial Branch

A Nonpartisan Force

South Carolina's judicial history has been buried in relative obscurity. Unlike the legislative and executive branches of government, whose histories have been well documented, no comprehensive books have been written examining the judiciary's evolution in the state.[1] However documents, essays, and academic research do exist that give us an idea of how the judiciary's structure and operations have evolved over time. And the courts' impact on the individual lives of South Carolinians has assuredly been profound from the colonial era until today. While most citizens will never serve in the legislature or be appointed to an executive position, almost all will be called for jury duty, get a traffic ticket, or otherwise be direct participants in the state's legal system.

Before taking a quick look at the history of South Carolina's judiciary and its current operations, it is worth exploring the character of one of its greatest chief justices in the modern era, Justice Jean Hoefer Toal.

Chief Justice Jean Hoefer Toal

Madam Chief Justice Jean Hoefer Toal is a person of firsts: the first woman to chair a legislative standing committee; the first native Columbian, the first Roman Catholic, and the first woman to serve on the state's supreme court; and the first woman elected as chief justice of that court.[2]

Jean Toal seemed born a fighter. Early in life she became interested in the civil rights movement and stood shoulder to shoulder during her college years with the few White native South

FIGURE 5. Representative Jean Toal, 1979. Photograph by Vic Tutte. Copyright © The State Media Company. All rights reserved. For more information, contact the Walker Local and Family History Center at Richland Library, Columbia, SC 29201.

Carolinians who participated in the movement. After college Toal became one of only four women attending the University of South Carolina School of Law. When she graduated in 1968, she became the eleventh woman then actively practicing law in the entire state. Women were not even allowed to serve on state juries until the year before she graduated.

After law school Toal did not shy away from controversial legal representation while also creating a lucrative career. One notable case involved a suit against the South Carolina Senate, which banned women from serving as pages. Toal represented future lawyer Victoria Eslinger who had been appointed as a page by her local senator and denied the position by the Senate clerk because of her gender. Toal partnered with national attorneys, including Ruth Bader Ginsburg, in the federal suit, successfully fighting off state Senate arguments that, among other duties, women pages may have to deliver messages to senators in their hotel rooms, creating an appearance of impropriety. Although Eslinger and her team lost before the federal district court, they were successful on appeal, changing the South Carolina Senate forever. Toal also represented the Catawba Indian tribe, engaged in neighborhood politics, and was appointed by progressive governor John Carl West of Camden to the recently created Human Affairs Commission.

In 1974, Republicans were just starting to make a push into the South with Richard Nixon's Southern Strategy. Toal decided to take on a Republican incumbent state House member, Roger Kirk, in her affluent district. After a tireless campaign she emerged victorious and quickly became a force in the South Carolina House of Representatives.

During the 1970s and early 1980s, South Carolina's government experienced a rare surge of progressive racial and modernizing economic policies and leadership. Toal would be at the forefront of these efforts with a group of like-minded progressives including Bob McFadden of York, Bob Sheheen of Camden, Harriet Keyserling of Beaufort, Malloy McEachin of Florence, Ginger Crocker of Laurens, and several others. The group dubbed themselves the "Crazy Caucus." They socialized, ate together, plotted strategy, and planned to change the state. Their efforts led to increased home rule for local governments, increased transparency in government, judicial reform, legislative modernization, environmental protections, education financing, consumer protections, and much more. Known for her quick wit, cutting strategies, sharp debate skills, and team-building loyalty, Toal eventually would chair the Rules Committee and lead a bruising and unsuccessful fight to pass the federal Equal Rights Amendment, which would have enshrined equal rights for women in the United States Constitution.

Toal soon turned her attention to her dream of becoming a state supreme court justice. Only one woman had been elected to the judiciary by the General Assembly, Family Court Judge Judy Bridges (now Judy Bridges McMahon), whom Toal had helped elect in 1983. In 1984, Toal ran for the supreme court along with Circuit Court Judge Ernest Finney, who was seeking to become the first

Black South Carolina Supreme Court Justice since Reconstruction.[3] A third candidate in the race was Circuit Court Judge Lee Chandler. Chandler built a winning coalition of legislators and was elected, beating the sitting legislator Jean Toal along with the trailblazing judge Ernest Finney. Another supreme court seat came open for election the following year, and Toal and Finney again announced as candidates. The growing Legislative Black Caucus strongly supported Judge Finney, and he emerged as a consensus candidate among many legislators. Toal withdrew from the race stating, "Ernest and I represent the dreams and aspirations of many South Carolinians who have previously had only limited opportunities for public service."[4] Jean Toal may have lost her second race for the supreme court in as many years, but she was never a quitter.

In 1988, yet another seat came open for election to the state supreme court, and Jean Toal again announced her interest. Her Crazy Caucus friends rallied around her candidacy. The race would be a brutal contest between sitting circuit court judge Rodney A. Peeples and Toal. Judge Peeples was known for his rough-and-tumble personality along with strong legislative connections. Further stacking the odds against Toal was that since 1954 no state supreme court justice had been elected without first serving on a lower court. The calculations changed however when Peeples was not recommended by the judicial screening committee tasked with evaluating the qualifications of the candidates. Peeples later withdrew from the race in part because of ethics allegations. Jean Toal was lauded as "squeaky clean." When installed in office Toal referenced her "prayers" (hopes) to be worthy of the position and to become "known as a strict constructionist of the constitution with a high regard for individual rights."[5] Toal took office in early 1988, and friends hung a pink ribbon banner on the imposing columns of the South Carolina Supreme Court reading, "It's a girl!"

Toal's service on the court would be transformative, not just because of the decisions she joined in making, but because of her successful modernizing efforts on the court and as its chief justice.

Toal became known as sympathetic to the causes of children, tough on crime, a critic of video poker gambling, friendly to consumer rights, and a leader in annunciating a student's state constitutional right to an adequate education. One of Toal's greatest legacies was the modernization of court practices and procedures. As an associate justice, Toal helped to modernize the court's use of staff and its opinion writing. As chief justice she almost single-handedly led the effort to computerize court proceedings, records, and filings. She wisely determined to use cloud computing when such a thing was just emerging, and she forced local courts and counties to operate off the same platforms to truly unify and integrate the judicial system from top to bottom.

Unlike most South Carolina Supreme Court justices, Toal faced reelection opponents. Whether this was because of her creative disruption, her politics, her gender, or a mix of all three is hard to say. Toal was feared and loved, and she was always aware of the possible threats to her position. Her judicial decisions avoided the stereotypical labels of conservative or liberal. Her canny political instincts led her to carefully cultivate her legislative relationships throughout her career, and thus she always emerged victorious, once even aided by the support of the Right to Life movement. As a lawyer, legislator, justice, and chief justice, Toal managed to stay true to her practical progressive roots while never being pigeonholed into one camp or another. Madam Chief Justice changed South Carolina.

Evolution of the South Carolina Courts

South Carolina's courts date back to the colonial era and were some of the first to develop in what would become the United States. The state's minimal court structure of the colonial era looked very different from the system we have today.

The Colonial Era: Birth of a Court

Early government in colonial South Carolina was unified, with executive, legislative, and judicial functions overlapping and intermixed.[6]

During the proprietary era, the governor and Grand Council appointed by the Lords Proprietors handled almost all government functions. The council's powers included the judicial power, which was broadly exercised for offenses ranging from turkey theft to treason. By 1682, a county court had been created to handle civil matters, and in 1698 a chief justice was appointed over a general court for the entire colony. The chief justice was a member of the Grand Council and presided over all trials with appeals going to the council. This arrangement meant that appeals from the chief justice's decisions went to a council on which he also sat. Most early chief justices were not trained attorneys, with the notable exception of Chief Justice Nicholas Trott, who was appointed in 1703. Chief Justice Trott codified the colony's laws and has been called the "father" of the South Carolina court system.

After the South Carolina Revolution of 1719, the courts were restructured in a more coherent fashion. A chief justice continued to serve but was joined by four assistant justices. Unlike today's chief justice and justices of the state supreme court, these judges acted primarily as trial judges, conducting trials and ruling on everyday disputes. The chief justice was usually an Englishman and an attorney, while the assistant justices were South Carolinians "recommended solely by their integrity and common sense."[7]

South Carolina was at the forefront of judicial activism during the colonial era. Some of the first American conflicts between judicial and legislative bodies occurred in the state. In 1726, the Commons House protested the court's overruling of an act of the assembly. In this conflict we again see the intermixing of the branches of government, as Chief Justice Thomas Hepworth was also a member of the assembly and attempted to defend the court's decision there. In a reminder of the state's and nation's recurring and present-day political conflicts, the assembly passed a resolution rebuking the courts for unjustly asserting the concept of judicial review of legislative enactments. Conflicts between the courts and the assembly continued into the 1730s and 1740s, with the royally appointed chief justices, almost all Englishmen, becoming objects of hatred and derision by the colonists and assembly. These conflicts in part laid the groundwork for South Carolina's support of the American Revolution in the 1770s.

The courts' refusal to regularly sit in any part of South Carolina except Charles Town also led to great unrest as the population multiplied across the Backcountry. The Regulator movement of the 1760s (discussed in chapter 1) was in part an effort to informally provide law enforcement and administer justice in parts of the state in which court sessions were not regularly held. During the colonial period appellate courts did not exist separate from the trial courts as we know them today. Early on the appellate function was exercised by the Grand Council, and over time the appellate function was fulfilled by annual meetings of the trial judges themselves sitting as a "court of appeals."

The Revolutionary Era: Change Is on the Way

South Carolina's assertion of independence in 1776 resulted in a transformation of the court system, which continues to affect the state to this day. Recognizing the state's deep distrust of consolidated power and love of the people's branch of government, the Constitution of 1776 enshrined selection of judges in the legislative branch. Legislative selection of judges continues to this day, uninterrupted through times of war, federal occupation, the rise of Reconstruction officeholders, the White backlash, and into modern times.

At the time of American independence, nine of the thirteen states selected their judges by gubernatorial appointment while four provided for legislative election. Furthermore nine of the states, including South Carolina, allowed for lifetime appointment of judges during good behavior. And as with most of the country and Britain, South Carolina had separate courts for questions of law and equity. Historically courts of equity involved requests for relief other than money damages, such as injunctions or specific performance of a contract, and focused less on strict application of the law and more on equitable principles of justice. For years legal reformers griped about the artificial divisions between the two areas of law. Judges in both the law courts of general jurisdiction and the equity Chancery Court were chosen by the General Assembly. For most of this period separate appellate courts did not exist, and instead appeals were heard by trial judges sitting together to consider questions of law and equity.

Much like the federal Constitution the 1790 South Carolina Constitution left the formation of the judiciary up to the legislative branch. The General Assembly would decide how many judges existed, their pay, and much of their jurisdiction. The state constitution did provide however that judges would hold office for life "during good behavior." The prestige of a judgeship in South Carolina at that time is perhaps best demonstrated by the example of John Rutledge. In 1791, he was selected as an associate justice of the United States Supreme Court. He resigned that position to serve four years as South Carolina's chief justice, holding trials and hearing cases because no state supreme court yet existed. Justice Rutledge was then selected as chief justice of the United States Supreme Court, serving until his nomination was rejected by the US Senate.

While on the bench, Justice Rutledge declared an act of the General Assembly unconstitutional. This decision began the establishment of judicial review of legislative acts in South Carolina and was one of the first such judicial assertions in the entire nation. Over the next decade, South Carolina courts would again strike down acts of the General Assembly when the courts determined the General Assembly had overstepped legal boundaries.

The General Assembly also addressed the consolidation of judicial power in Charleston and lack of regular court hearings in the Backcountry by passing the Circuit Court Act of 1796. This act divided the state into seven districts and provided for regular court sessions. The state's court system would continue, mostly unchanged, with minor alterations to appellate court procedures until the Civil War.

The Reconstruction Era: Legislative Selection Survives

Reconstruction would see fundamental change in the court system of South Carolina. But one basic element would continue through federal occupation, the rise of Black elected officials, the Conservative White backlash, the rural White Reform movement, and the modern era: the legislative selection of judges.

The Constitutional Convention of 1868 was dominated by Black and Republican delegates. This constitution is the only South Carolina Constitution to ever be voted on in toto by its registered voters. During the convention debate some delegates proposed selection of judges based on the federal model of executive appointment. Some delegates supported popular election of judges. But in the end the delegates rejected these proposals and stuck with election of judges by "the people's' branch" of government, the General Assembly.

Several critical changes in the judiciary were made in this new constitution, changes which survive to this day. First, the South Carolina Supreme Court was created. This court was made up of three members. The supreme court was empowered to hear appeals in both law and equity. The constitutional creation of a supreme court strengthened the judiciary as a third constitutionally recognized branch of government. Second, lifetime appointment of judges was abolished. Jonathon Jasper Wright, who would become the first Black member of the South Carolina Supreme Court argued fiercely against lifetime appointments, citing the decisions of the lifelong justices of the United States Supreme Court that disempowered Black citizens.[8] Instead six-year terms of office were set for the state judges.

The Constitution of 1868 was also more detailed in explaining how inferior courts should work, requiring written opinions in certain matters, allowing the use of court reporters, and empowering clerks of court. Separate courts for equity and law were abolished, and instead the courts of common pleas and general sessions were created to hear civil and criminal cases. These courts continue to operate today.

Period of Conservative Bourbon Restoration and Tillman's White Reformer Backlash

The new judiciary structure remained fairly stable during Reconstruction. And the basic designs survived both the Bourbon Restoration of White conservatives and the subsequent White Reform backlash. It is important to recall that the initial post-Reconstruction White supremacy effort was led by the traditional White Conservative leadership under Wade Hampton, referred to as the Bourbons, hearkening back to the French aristocracy and the Southern whiskey. This Bourbon leadership was generally content with the structural changes in the judiciary created by the Reconstruction government. Nevertheless the most fundamental change in the South Carolina judicial system during these years was the purging of Black and Republican members from the judiciary through impeachment efforts and refusal to reelect them to the bench, including the attempted impeachment of the first Black justice, Justice Wright. The structure of the judiciary may have been stable during this time, but the occupancy of those positions and the politics surrounding the officeholders was anything but calm.

Upon the ascension of the White Tillmanites to the legislature and executive branches, Tillman and his team set about removing White Conservative judges from the judiciary and replacing them with even more Tillmanites. Much of this effort revolved around Governor Tillman's plans to create a state-run alcohol dispensary, a fascinating topic in itself. The state supreme court initially ruled this plan unconstitutional. However it reversed itself after the Tillman faction successfully led the effort to replace an anti-Tillman member of the supreme court, whose term had expired, with a Tillmanite justice.

Amazingly the Constitution of 1895 did not fundamentally alter the judicial structure of the Reconstruction Constitution of 1868. It did however add a fourth seat to the supreme court, creating the potential for an impasse on the court, but including a tie-breaking mechanism that included all circuit court judges. It also extended the terms of the justices to staggered eight-year periods. And again this new constitution enshrined the election of judges by joint vote of the General Assembly.

The Modern Era: Streamlining Justice

Important changes in the judiciary have occurred since the nineteenth century. Through amendment the constitution was changed to allow for five members of the supreme court, a number that remains today.

Informal but critically important traditions have come to define the state's courts in many ways. For example, for the better part of a century the General Assembly has elected the most senior associate justice to become the chief justice when such an opening arises.[9] This tradition has held true even when the chief justice previously held elective office in the political minority party. Such stability has allowed the state supreme court and the courts in general to avoid political and partisan maneuvering or typecasting. Unlike many states and increasingly in the federal government, courts in South Carolina are still viewed as generally nonpartisan.

Further providing stability in the court system has been the General Assembly's recognition that, although not statutorily required, judges with a few exceptions have been reelected absent allegations of incompetence, scandal, or other bad behavior. This tradition has created a de facto service of judges until retirement at age seventy-two as long as they exhibit good behavior. Also fostering stability and a nonpartisan judiciary has been the more than two centuries old selection method for judges, which will be discussed further below.

Although the South Carolina state courts were generally not friendly places for civil rights efforts in the 1950s and '60s, the federal courts and judges played an important role. National efforts to integrate schools arose in the state when Black parents filed the case of *Briggs v. Elliot* in rural Clarendon County. The case would be combined into the famous *Brown v. Board of Education* decision of the United State Supreme Court outlawing segregated public schools. One of three federal judges who heard the Briggs case on the district level was South Carolinian J. Waites Waring. Although he was in the minority in that case, his statement in dissent that "segregation is per se inequality" would have an effect on the supreme court's ultimate decision.

Judge Waring was a White judicial appointee of Franklin Roosevelt who had come up through the South Carolina Democratic establishment. When exposed to racial inequalities during his career, he became a progressive on racial issues, ruling that all-White Democratic primaries were illegal and that Black citizens deserved the opportunity to attend a state-supported law school. He stated that "the cancer of segregation will never be cured by the sedative of gradualism."[10]

Tremendous structural change came to the South Carolina court system in the early 1970s. Over time the trial courts had become a hodgepodge of jurisdictions and noncoordination. Over the years to help with growing dockets, the General Assembly had created "county courts" in some counties, while allowing the circuit courts to handle all matters in others. The result was overlapping jurisdictions and confusion. Lacking administrative power, the supreme court had little influence over local courts except the review of legal decisions, and the system was extremely decentralized, inconsistent, and had little conformity. The national Institute of Judicial Administration stated that South Carolina's court system "defies classification."[11]

In the early 1970s an effort by the state bar and a small group of progressive legislators resulted in a constitutional amendment reforming the structure of the judiciary to be proposed to voters. In 1972, this amendment was adopted and a "unified court system" was created. One result was the creation of a new separate system of family courts. The amendment broadly required a unified system with consistent legal procedures and uniform avenues for appeals. It left the details of implementation to the General Assembly. In the end this effort would empower the state supreme court to set rules for judicial process, provide administration to the courts, and have budgetary control over court personnel and expenditures. In essence the changes allowed the third branch of government to finally become self-governing.

Even after the constitutional amendment was passed, creating a uniform, independent judiciary did not come easily. For a period of time the General Assembly continued to assert the right to make the rules of court and was rebutted by the South Carolina Supreme Court in several decisions. The General Assembly and the state supreme court fought for the better part of a decade over everything from who got to set court rules to the election of judges to the creation of a court of appeals. In 1975, the supreme court struck down twenty-nine statutes the General Assembly passed by ruling that they did not comply with the newly adopted requirement of a unified court system. Finally in 1984 a truce developed, a court of appeals was created through constitutional amendment, and the supreme court's power over the judiciary was cemented.

Through the efforts of civil rights advocates, the state's courts gradually became populated by a more diverse population starting in the 1980s and '90s. Although the state's supreme court currently has no Black members, it has had two Black chief justices in the years spanning 1994 to 2014. Several women have served on the state's supreme court, including a lengthy tenure by Justice Toal as chief justice. And many Black and female judges have served and continue to serve as judges throughout the court systems of South Carolina.

Appellate Courts: The Final Appeal

Appellate courts are the bodies that hear appeals from trial courts, whether criminal or civil. Their development in South Carolina was slow and fitful and continued into the late 1900's.

Development of Appellate Courts

The concept of appellate courts, including rule-making authority, as we know them today, was absent from the South Carolina judiciary during the 1700s and much of the 1800s. Instead appeals from decisions of the trial judges were heard by all the trial judges sitting as a group.

In 1808, the General Assembly created a three-judge court of appeals, but only to hear appeals from equity cases. Appeals of legal questions continued to be heard by trial judges who assembled as a whole. Finally in 1824, a true court of appeals was created to hear appeals from both courts of law and courts of equity. This court of appeals would not last for long; it became a victim to the sectional politics of nullification. In the 1830s, John C. Calhoun's concept of distinct state nullification of federal law reached a high-water mark. South Carolina's own native son, President Andrew Jackson, pushed back vehemently. The state was divided between Unionists, who supported the primacy of the federal government, and Nullifiers, who supported states' rights. Questions of race and slavery lurked not far beneath the surface.

Amid this national dispute, the General Assembly statutorily passed a law in 1833 requiring a "test oath" of every military official swearing allegiance to the State of South Carolina. Unionists believed this oath denied allegiance to the nation. The dispute was a forerunner of the secession fight to come. The South Carolina Court of Appeals struck down the test oath in 1834, supporting soldiers who refused to take the oath. In 1835, the court decided another case supporting the primacy of federal law. And later that year the General Assembly, having statutorily created the court, abolished the court of appeals. A mishmash of appellate courts was created and changed over the next couple of decades until the post–Civil War era brought a true appellate court system into being.

As mentioned above, the Reconstruction Constitution of 1868 saw fundamental change in the South Carolina appellate court system. For the first time a supreme court was created, and it would hear appeals in both law and equity. The supreme court consisted of three full-time justices, later increased to four, and finally increased to five in 1911. In basic structure the supreme court created in 1868 survives to this day, with growth in staff, jurisdiction, power, and functions.

Appellate Courts Today

Today the supreme court is the highest court in South Carolina. The chief justice is the administrative head of the entire judicial department. The justices are elected to staggered ten-year terms; terms were set at eight years, with the enlargement of the court to four justices, in 1895 and increased to ten years, with the addition of a fifth justice, in 1911. By tradition the most senior associate justice is elected chief justice when there is a vacancy. And by tradition justices are reelected by the General Assembly if their tenure is marked by good behavior. Partisanship has been noticeably absent from these processes in the modern era.

The supreme court exercises both appellate and limited original jurisdiction. The court can, at its discretion, hear appeals from the family and circuit courts and has sole appellate jurisdiction over the court of appeals. For the most part the supreme court may decide which appeals to take under consideration and which to decline to consider. However, appeals in cases involving the death penalty, public utility rates, public bond issuances, election laws, and the constitutionality of state laws are heard in the first instance by the supreme court. The court also sets the rules of the court, oversees the court system's administration, and handles budget and disciplinary matters.

The court of appeals is an intermediate appellate court that was created in 1983 to ease the caseload of appeals heard by the supreme court. Its membership initially consisted of six members and was subsequently raised to nine. The court hears appeals by sitting in three- judge panels. The court of appeals hears most appeals from the circuit courts, family courts, the administrative law court, and the Workers' Compensation Commission. Its decisions may be reviewed by the state supreme court. Its judges are elected by the General Assembly to staggered six-year terms.

The Lower Courts

Today the South Carolina Unified Court System has a number of lower courts. These courts include state circuit courts, state family courts, county magistrate courts, county probate courts, and municipal courts. Hybrid courts, such as the administrative law court and the Workers' Compensation Commission handle specialized administrative matters.

Circuit Courts: The Workhorses

The "workhorses" of the state's court system are the circuit or trial courts. Circuit court judges handle both civil and criminal cases. The civil division is called the court of common pleas. This division hears all civil cases, or lawsuits, that involve more than $7,500 in claims. Typical cases adjudicated by the court of common pleas include business litigation, contract disputes, personal injuries, and land disputes. Litigants are entitled to request that juries render a decision on the facts of the cases and enter a verdict for either the plaintiff or the defendant, while judges determine questions of law.

The criminal division is called the court of general sessions. This division hears felony charges as well as some more serious misdemeanor charges. Typical cases adjudicated by the court of general sessions include murder charges, drug trafficking, burglary, and felony DUI. Juries make decisions relating to the facts of the cases and render a verdict of guilty or not guilty. Judges render the sentences of the defendants, except in death penalty cases.

Circuit judges sit on both criminal and civil divisions. These judges are elected by the General Assembly to staggered six-year terms of office. They must be licensed attorneys for at least eight years, must be thirty-two years of age, and must have resided in the state for at least five years. It is customary that once judges are elected, they are reelected for as long as they wish to remain on the bench as long as no financial, legal, competency, or other scandal has emerged.

The state is divided into sixteen judicial circuits. Each circuit has at least one resident circuit judge. Some judges' seats are assigned to particular circuits, and occupants must live within those circuits. Other seats are considered "at large," and occupants may live in any part of the State. Forty-nine judges fill the circuit court and are assigned to cases throughout South Carolina on a rotating basis. Court terms and assignments are made by the chief justice of the supreme court based on recommendations of the court administration.

Family Courts: Family Disputes

In 1976, South Carolina's General Assembly created specialized family courts to hear all matters dealing with marriage, separation, divorce, child custody, name changes, and juvenile criminal allegations. This progressive change allowed such judges to specialize in matters pertaining to family and domestic situations. South Carolina was one of the earlier states to adopt a unified, comprehensive family court system, and some states still do not have such a system. Family courts in South Carolina operate without a jury, with the judges making all findings of fact and conclusions of law.

Family court judges are elected by the General Assembly for six-year terms. At least two family court judges are elected to each of the sixteen judicial circuits. These judges rotate primarily from county to county within their resident circuits. Occasionally they are assigned to other circuits as directed by the chief justice. Family court judges must meet the same age and residency requirements as circuit court judges.

Magistrate and Municipal Courts: Front Lines of Justice

Magistrate courts and municipal courts in South Carolina are also known as summary courts. Like circuit courts, magistrate courts have both civil and criminal jurisdiction. However, magistrate jurisdiction is limited to misdemeanor charges in criminal matters and claims involving $7,500 or less in civil matters. Magistrate judges can levy criminal penalties of imprisonment not exceeding thirty days or a fine of not more than $500. Magistrate judges also set bail, issue arrest and search warrants, impose restraining orders, and conduct preliminary hearings in criminal matters.

Magistrate court juries are empaneled in both criminal and civil trials. Typical criminal cases that a magistrate may hear include domestic violence, DUI, simple possession of marijuana, loitering, writing bad checks, or traffic offenses. Typical civil cases that a magistrate may hear include landlord-tenant matters, small breach of contract claims, and minor personal injuries.

Approximately three hundred magistrates are appointed in South Carolina. Senators in each county recommend persons to the governor for appointment for that county. By tradition governors appoint the persons recommended by the county senators unless legal, financial, or ethical improprieties exist. Magistrates may serve either part-time or full-time. Magistrates do not have to be attorneys, but they are required to have a four-year college degree. They must also pass a required examination.

South Carolina allows cities and towns to establish municipal courts if they so choose. Approximately two hundred municipalities have established courts to hear criminal offenses that occur within their jurisdictions. In criminal cases the powers and duties of municipal judges are the same as those of county magistrate judges. However municipal judges have no jurisdiction over civil cases. Cities that do not establish municipal courts may prosecute their criminal cases in the county magistrate system.

Probate Courts: Death and Marriage

Probate courts exist in each of the state's forty-six counties. They have jurisdiction over the estates of deceased persons, the issuance of marriage licenses, the appointment of guardians and conservators for minors or incompetent persons, involuntary commitments for mental-health reasons, disputes involving trusts, and approval of minor settlements under $25,000.

Probate courts are an outlier in South Carolina in that probate court judges are the only judges popularly elected by voters in each county. Probate judges also run on a partisan ballot, resulting in the ludicrous game of what a Republican probate judge's governing philosophy versus a Democratic judge's might be.

Selection of Judges: Tried and Survived

The method for selection of judges in South Carolina has been the subject of much debate, controversy, contumely, angst, and hysteria for almost a century. Throughout the nation there are a variety of ways that judges are selected. The federal model allows the executive branch to appoint judges for life with advice and consent of the United States Senate. North Carolina is one of many states that primarily uses popular, partisan elections. Some states have a mixture of these two methods. South Carolina is one of only two states that selects its statewide judges through election by the legislature.

Legislative selection of judges has been a core tenet of state government since South Carolina signed the Declaration of Independence in 1776. The selection process has undergone many changes. For example up until the 1990s, sitting legislators were regularly elected directly from the legislative body to the courts at which time they would resign from the legislature and be sworn in as judges. For much of the twentieth century this process created a judiciary primarily made up of former legislators.

Supporters of electing legislators to the bench argued that doing so ensured persons were vetted both through public election (legislative elections) and an eventual judicial selection process. Supporters also argued that political representation on the bench was important to bring communication, negotiation, and other life skills to bear in the administration of justice. Opponents of legislators being elected to judicial office directly from the legislature argued that the practice precluded nonlegislators from being competitively considered for the judiciary, was incestuous, resulted in incompetent judges, and smacked of conflicts of interest.

This dispute reached a boiling point in the 1990s, and over time the opponents' viewpoint became dominant in the public and General Assembly. In 1996, a judicial reform amendment was submitted to and approved by voters. Sitting legislators were barred from being elected to the bench, and the Judicial Merit Selection Commission was formed to vet qualifications of applicants before the General Assembly voted on them. The commission is made up of a combination of members of the General Assembly and laypersons. These changes have led to an opening of the judiciary to lawyers from a variety of backgrounds and an overall improvement in the bench in South Carolina. A stable, nonpartisan judiciary has emerged that has generally avoided many of the partisan problems and scandals seen in other states.

Because South Carolina is an outlier in how it selects judges, its selection method often comes under attack. However the process of legislative selection avoids serious pitfalls associated with executive selection or popular appointment. Executive selection is nontransparent, with decisions being made by a governor with little to no input from other than the governor's advisers. Judicial appointments in an executive system are often made based on financial or political support made to the governor. Furthermore, partisanship has become a touchstone of executive appointment as is increasingly seen on the national level. Popular elections often result in hyperpartisanship in judicial races, the massive empowering of political donors in the judicial system, and dominance in selection by corporate and legal interests.

Legislative election, while not without faults, has tended to result in the selection of nonpartisan judges who must cobble together support from legislators in both parties to be elected. Controversy and extreme positions are not winning approaches to judicial selection in South Carolina. The candidates are vetted by the Judicial Merit Selection Commission for competency and then considered by 170 separately elected members of the General Assembly. Elections are held in public joint session of the House and Senate with any arguments for or against being aired publicly. Campaign money and fund-raising are notably absent from the system, and corruption scandals in the judiciary are minuscule compared to those in other states. It is often said that South Carolina "has the worst selection method for judges except for all the other methods."

Other Court Officers and Institutions

The administration of justice in South Carolina requires a number of other officers and institutions. Among these are countywide elected clerks of court who manage the courthouse, provide staff for the courts' local administrative duties, assemble juries, handle fines and fees, maintain court records, handle child support payment, and other duties. Clerks of court are elected on a countywide partisan basis and serve four-year terms.

Prosecutors in South Carolina are known as solicitors. Solicitors and their assistant attorneys prosecute almost all felony criminal cases as well as some serious misdemeanors in the state. Solicitors are elected from each judicial district on a partisan basis and serve four-year terms.

Public defenders are provided to indigent persons by the state in all felony cases as well as misdemeanor cases that are likely to result in the imposition of a prison sentence. Public defenders are hired by boards established within each judicial district.

Masters in Equity mainly handle foreclosures and other matters dealing with property ownership in each county. They may also hear other civil cases referred to them by the circuit courts, usually with the consent of the parties. Masters in Equity serve six-year terms and are selected by each county's state legislators, who make a recommendation to the governor.

Quietly, competently, and in a nonpartisan manner, South Carolina's judiciary impacts the lives of the state's citizens. A powerful chief justice of the state supreme court now has the ability to influence all the state's courts through administrative policy and court precedent. Although it has been tweaked and changed, legislative selection of judges has survived in every constitution and governmental type since the state's founding.

5

Important State Agencies

Meeting the Needs of a Growing State

The complexity and growth of modern society have been matched in South Carolina by the growth and complexity of its state government functions and the agencies necessary to carry out those tasks. Any discussion of state government agencies risks getting bogged down in the necessary minutiae of day-to-day work, overlapping activities, and confusing names. This chapter will briefly discuss almost all of South Carolina's agencies, focusing on those that are large or frequently affect its citizens. The agencies are alphabetized by type (Arts and History, Business, Regulatory, and Transportation, and so forth) and then listed alphabetically within the type. There are also many small state boards or commissions that may be filled only by volunteers and may fall under the umbrella of larger state agencies. A complete listing of all these entities is virtually impossible and will not be attempted here.

To begin the foray into the complexities of South Carolina's ever-evolving and ever-changing state agency structure, we will look back in time to one of the most combative showdowns in state-agency history.

DOT and Machine Gun Olin

No state agency touches the daily lives of South Carolinians more than the Department of Transportation (DOT), and perhaps no government service is taken more for granted than its product: our roads.[1] Because of South Carolina's history of top-down governance, the State Department of Transportation controls more road miles than all but three states, with more than 41,000 miles.

FIGURE 6. *Olin D. Johnston, 1956. Copyright © The State Media Company. All rights reserved. For more information, contact the Walker Local and Family History Center at Richland Library, Columbia, SC 29201.*

The South Carolina DOT maintains more miles of road than the Georgia and Florida departments combined. Most states have a richer and longer history of local governments, which allowed for roadways to be developed and maintained by those local governments, instead of by the states. South Carolina's emphasis on state-level control has meant that the Department of Transportation has played an outsized role in state government and politics since its creation in the early 1900s.

Originally known as the State Highway Commission, the agency was founded in 1917 by Governor Richard I. Manning and composed of five members. It was more formalized in 1920, when the General Assembly created a seven-member commission appointed by the governor and confirmed by the Senate. The agency grew rapidly as dirt, farm-to-market roads were paved and major highways built.

Governor Olin D. Johnston was a shockingly colorful character, intimately involved in the development of the State DOT and its roadways.[2] Hailing from Anderson County he grew up working on the family farm and in local textile mills. He represented and emerged from a new interest in the state, that of the blue-collar millworker. Rough-and-ready like the mills in which he grew up and worked, Olin Johnston fought in the trenches of South Carolina politics his entire life. As governor he reversed the policy of using national guard troops to break workers' strikes and instead used the military force to protect strikers and embargo strikebreakers. Economically liberal while racially conservative he maintained the philosophy of White supremacy that undergirded the cultural norms of South Carolina while pushing reforms to help poor Whites in the state.

Governor Johnson's greatest conflict centered around the State Highway Commission.[3] Not long after taking office as governor in 1935, Johnston tried to dismiss members of the Highway Commission to make his own appointments. Backed by legislators, the commissioners flatly refused to leave office. So in October 1935, Johnston imposed martial law, accused commissioners of rebellion and insurrection, and ordered the National Guard to occupy the agency and seize control. The Guard, armed with machine guns, stormed the building and established physical control. Governor Johnston demanded that the seated commissioners resign unless they agreed to work "loyally and faithfully." The siege lasted two months, at which time the legislature compromised with the governor by agreeing in an emergency session to give control of the agency to a "provisional board."

But the staying power of legislative supremacy was hard to beat, even by a governor as strong-willed and colorful as Johnston. Ultimately the legislature stripped the power to appoint commissioners from the governor and vested it in the legislative body. That appointment power remained legislative even as the agency changed and grew over more than seventy years. That power returned to the governor's office in another compromise between the legislature and governor's office enacted under Act 40 in 2017.

Olin Johnston was from then on known as "Machine Gun

Olin." And the South Carolina Department of Transportation has remained in the spotlight of political and popular debate for most of its existence.

Arts and History

South Carolina has had a strong cultural attachment to its history and its arts. Starting in the early 1900s and continuing until today, state institutions have developed and grown to protect and promote the state's history and arts, often with controversy.

Department of Archives and History

The commission is appointed by the governor and confirmed by the Senate as well as institutional members. The commission hires a director. Duties include the preservation of the documentary history of South Carolina, administration of grants relating to historic properties, and administration of the African American Heritage Commission. The department has a fascinating collection of South Carolina's most treasured documents, including many of its constitutions, most of which had been neglected over the years. For example, the Constitution of 1776 was found by the famous senator Edgar Brown in the early 1940s moldering in a dusty statehouse storeroom before being preserved by the department.[4]

Arts Commission

The commission is appointed by the governor and confirmed by the Senate. The commission hires a director. The mission of the Arts Commission is the promotion of equitable access to the arts and to support creativity in South Carolina. The Arts Commission survived attempts by Governors Nikki Haley[5] and Mark Sanford[6] to abolish its mission when each governor vetoed the commission's budget. Legislators who valued the arts in South Carolina overrode the vetoes keeping the commission's works to support the continuation of arts in the state.

Confederate Relic Room Commission

Commission members are appointed by the governor, the president of the Senate, and the Speaker of the House. The commission controls the Confederate Relic Room, which is the third oldest museum in the state and exhibits important historical artifacts related to the state's military history. The Confederate Relic Room initially existed within the statehouse itself but is now housed next to the State Museum. Even the name of the Confederate Relic Room has spurred controversy, and it now houses the Confederate battle flag removed from the statehouse grounds in 2015.

State Library

The commission is appointed by the governor. The South Carolina State Library is the primary administrator of federal and state support for the state's libraries. It has responsibility for public library development, library service for state institutions, service for the blind and physically handicapped, and library service to state government agencies. Two impressive statues of lions grace the State Library's entranceway. The lions originally framed the entrance to the Court Inn, a prominent hotel retreat that existed in the city of Camden during its "Hotel Era" of the early 1900s when Camden was a tourist destination for wealthy Northerners with elegant hotels in which to winter.

State Museum

The commission is appointed by the governor. The commission hires a director. It is charged with creating and operating a museum highlighting the history, fine arts, natural history, and industrial history of the state. It is located in Columbia. The State Museum is a South Carolina gem.

Business, Regulatory, and Transportation

In the modern era agencies have been formed to both regulate and promote business and commercial interests. State agencies attempt to encourage the growth of business while setting many rules within which business must operate. State agencies also help provide the necessary infrastructure in transportation and energy necessary for a modern economy.

Department of Commerce

The director is appointed by the governor, confirmed by the Senate, and considered part of the governor's cabinet. The department provides services relating to business recruitment, economic and tax incentives, and workforce training. This agency plays a high-profile role in recruiting foreign and out-of-state corporations to locate branch facilities in South Carolina. It has sometimes been criticized as perpetuating a "sharecrop" mentality of economic development by recruiting out-of-state companies with promises of low taxes, low wages, and cheap land instead of nurturing successful South Carolina businesses, resulting in an inability to build wealth much like that faced by early 1900s "sharecroppers," who could only rent land to subsistence farm therefore rarely got ahead. The approach brings needed jobs but rarely creates generational wealth.

Department of Insurance

The director is appointed by the governor, confirmed by the Senate, and considered part of the governor's cabinet. The department licenses and provides oversight of insurance companies operating within the state, assists in resolving insurance-related complaints, investigates allegations of insurance fraud, and collects and releases relevant data.

Department of Labor, Licensing, and Regulation

The director is appointed by the governor, confirmed by the Senate, and considered part of the governor's cabinet. Groups administered by the agency include such boards as the Athletic Commission, Real Estate Commission, Medical Examiners, and the Cemetery Board. Department of Labor, Licensing, and Regulation is sometimes referred to as a "smorgasbord" agency, in that legislators "park" programs there for administration when they do not otherwise know where to place them.

Department of Motor Vehicles

The director is appointed by the governor, confirmed by the Senate, and considered part of the governor's cabinet. The department handles most issues relating to automobile driving and vehicles in the state, including driver's and vehicle licensing. The department moved from being one of the most hated and dysfunctional agencies in the 1980s to a relatively efficient operation by the early 2000s.

Ports Authority

The commission is appointed by the governor and confirmed by the Senate. The commission hires a director. The port of Charleston has been a major driver in the economy of South Carolina for generations as well as the very reason the city was established. Commission positions are highly sought after in the business and political communities.

Public Service Authority–Santee Cooper Utility

The commission is appointed by the governor and confirmed by the Senate. The commission hires a director. The authority's primary duty is the operation of the Santee Cooper power facilities and the management of Lakes Marion and Moultrie. The authority has been a controversial point in recent years due in large part to the billions of dollars lost in a failed nuclear power plant construction project.[7]

Department of Transportation

Board members are appointed by the governor with approval from the legislators for each district. The department manages, repairs, and constructs most roads within South Carolina. Unlike most states in which local governments maintain roads, South Carolina's state government owns, operates, and maintains most roads within its borders. In 2017, South Carolina passed its single biggest tax increase ever and dedicated new gas tax proceeds to road repairs and construction. This author proudly chaired the Senate and conference committees that drafted and passed the legislation.[8]

Conservation and Environmental

Although historically a rural state, South Carolina has seen rapid development in the latter part of the twentieth and early part of the twenty-first centuries. A love of the land has manifested itself in many policies and decisions in South Carolina politics, leading to the formation of agencies charged with protecting natural resources and providing for public use and enjoyment. This land ethic often conflicts with South Carolina's equally powerful dedication to business growth.

Conservation Bank

The board is appointed by the governor, the president of the Senate, and the Speaker of the House. The board hires its agency director. The bank funds the preservation of and public access to wildlife habitats, natural areas, historical sites, sites of unique ecological significance, forests, farmlands, watersheds, open space, and urban parks. Notable among its many successes are thousands of acres preserved from development along Lake Wateree and the Savannah River.

Department of Environmental Services

The department head is appointed by the governor and confirmed by the Senate. Until 2024, the Department of Environmental Services was part of the very large Department of Health and Environmental Control (DHEC). In that year the environmental services functions were carved out of DHEC and established in a new agency. The agency handles environmental permitting, compliance, and protection.[9]

Forestry Commission

The commission is appointed by the governor and confirmed by the Senate. The commission hires the state forester. The commission is charged with protecting and enhancing the state's forests. It achieves those goals in two primary ways. First, it operates and manages the state-owned forests, most notably Sandhills State Forest located primarily in Chesterfield County. Second, its staff fights forest fires, assists private landowners in forest management, and promulgates best forestry practices throughout the state. As the state's private farming acres have shrunk, its private-forestry plantings have increased, and this agency's mission has taken on new life.

Department of Natural Resources

The commission is appointed by the governor and confirmed by the Senate. The commission hires a director. The department's scope is wide. Among other responsibilities it conserves and manages lands within the state, provides and licenses hunting and fishing opportunities for citizens, conducts environmental and biological research, recommends game limits, manages wildlife success, and provides law enforcement officers (game wardens) to enforce hunting and fishing laws. The Department of Natural Resources has emerged as a steady and powerful force in forest and wetland conservation in South Carolina, working to protect thousands of acres.

Parks, Recreation, and Tourism

The director is appointed by the governor, confirmed by the Senate, and considered part of the governor's cabinet. The SC Parks, Recreation, and Tourism operates and manages South Carolina's forty-seven state parks, markets the state as a preferred vacation destination, and assists communities in developing recreation assets. It emerged during the latter part of the twentieth century as a major player in the economy of South Carolina.

Education

Since the Constitution of 1868, education has been a focus of state government in South Carolina. Over the years education agencies have been formed to keep up with technological advancement and changing priorities. State and local governments in South Carolina spend by far the largest portion of public dollars on education.

South Carolina Department of Education

The mission of the South Carolina Department of Education is to provide leadership and support so that all public education students graduate prepared for success. It achieves these efforts primarily through support of local school districts. Among its many duties the agency distributes state funds to districts, handles procurement of statewide education services, and manages statewide educational data and programs. The agency is led by the state superintendent of education.

State Board of Education

The State Board of Education is established in Article XI, Section 1 of the South Carolina Constitution. The board consists of seventeen members, one appointed from each of the state's sixteen judicial circuits by the legislators representing the various circuits, and a seventeenth member appointed by the governor. Members are appointed for four-year terms. Among its duties the board adopts statewide education policy, determines curriculum policy, votes on regulations, and hears matters involving educator employment. The board is supported in its mission by the Department of Education.

Educational Television Commission

The commission is appointed by the governor and confirmed by the Senate. The commission hires a director. South Carolina has historically had a well-recognized ETV program that both creates and disseminates educational television and radio material. South Carolina was an early pioneer in public television, and SCETV is respected around the country, producing programs that are syndicated in many markets on both television and public radio.

First Steps Board of Trustees

The board is made up of a complex membership, sharing power between the executive and legislative branches. The General Assembly established First Steps in 1999 upon the urging of Governor Jim Hodges to close the gap in students' preparedness for success in school. The agency offers a wide array of services that improves children's health, strengthens families, expands access to quality early care and education, and helps transition rising kindergartners into school. Perhaps most important to note, it is tasked with implementing and coordinating state-funded private four-year-old kindergarten programs throughout the state.

Commission on Higher Education

The commission is governed by a board of fifteen members appointed by the governor. Four are statewide at-large members, with one appointed as chair; one member from each of the state's seven congressional districts; three members who serve as college and university trustees, representing the public colleges and universities; and one nonvoting ex officio member who serves as president of a private independent college. Members representing congressional districts are appointed by the governor upon recommendation of many of the state senators and House members who compose the district's legislative delegation. The remaining members are recommended and appointed on the advice and consent of the Senate. Commissioners serve four-year terms, except for the institutional representatives, who serve two-year terms. The commission hires a director.

The agency administers lottery-funded scholarships and grants, approves new academic degree programs, collects and reports on postsecondary education data, licenses private educational institutions operating in the state, recommends policy to the legislative and executive branches, and reviews the policies and operations of institutions of higher education.

Universities and Technical Colleges

The state owns twelve four-year universities and colleges. It also owns sixteen two-year technical colleges. Boards of trustees for the universities vary in size, and most board members are elected by the General Assembly, with some members appointed by the governor. State funding for universities in South Carolina has decreased dramatically over the last decade as a share of their operating expenses. Technical colleges also have boards of trustees of various sizes that are usually selected by local legislative delegations.

Government Support and Operations Services

For a state government to function it must have administrative support and technical expertise. Raising necessary taxes, reviewing its finances, enforcing its election laws, and much more goes into the operations of a functioning state government.

State Auditor

The state auditor is appointed by members of the State Fiscal Accountability Authority. The State Auditor's Office audits the state's comprehensive annual financial report and the state's annual schedule of expenditures of federal awards. It also provides auditing and other similar services to state agencies designed to meet regulatory and financial practice requirements. It has been suggested that the appointment of the state auditor should not rest with the State Fiscal Accountability Authority; the auditor is supposed to audit some of the members' offices such as the comptroller general, who is one of the state auditor's bosses.

Election Commission

Five members are appointed by the governor for four-year terms. The commission hires an executive director. At least one member must belong to the majority political party and at least one to the largest minority political party represented in the General Assembly. The commission is tasked with coordinating elections throughout the state and partners with local election commissions to run elections and register voters. The commission maintains records and handles election-related procurements. Traditionally this agency was operated by nonpartisan professionals, and the commission ensured that it stayed that way. As trends have changed nationally that mission has become harder to maintain.

Ethics Commission

Eight members make up the commission: four appointed by the governor, two selected by the House of Representatives, and two selected by the Senate. Minority party representation is required. The commission ensures compliance with the state's laws on financial and campaign disclosures; regulates lobbyists and lobbying organizations; issues advisory opinions; educates public officeholders and the public on the state's ethics laws; conducts criminal and administrative investigations of violations of the state's ethics laws; and prosecutes violators either administratively or criminally. While involved in the administering of the General Assembly's ethical

Important State Agencies 103

compliance, the Senate and House ethics committees make decisions relating to members' ethical violations to comply with separation of powers considerations. This agency has been the subject of innumerable fights about how best to enforce ethics laws while respecting the separation of powers.[10]

State Fiscal Accountability Authority

This important agency, State Fiscal Accountability Authority (SFAA), was created by the Restructuring Act of 2014.[11] That act abolished the powerful Budget and Control Board and vested its duties primarily in the newly created Department of Administration under the governor. The act also created the State Fiscal Affairs Authority to hold some powers that did not fit neatly into the executive or legislative branch. The SFAA is governed by a board that includes executive and legislative members: the governor, the treasurer, the comptroller general, the chair of the House Ways and Means Committee, and the chair of the Senate Finance Committee. The agency provides executive support for the Agency Head Salary Commission, the South Carolina Opioid Recovery Fund, and the agency's five-member governing board. The agency's board (the authority) provides fiscal oversight through its review and approval of major governmental undertakings, such as bonded indebtedness, transactions involving real property, permanent improvement projects, and certain litigation settlements. Fiscal accountability is also provided by the authority's oversight of the state's centralized auditing of state agency procurement operations and its management of the state auditor's centralized financial audits.

Public Employee Benefit Authority

The South Carolina Public Employee Benefit Authority (PEBA) was created in 2012 and is governed by an eleven-member board of directors that supervises and directs the agency's functions and hires the agency's leaders. PEBA's board of directors is composed of eleven appointed members. Board members are either representative, meaning they belong to a class of employees or retirees they represent, or nonrepresentative. Appointments are made by the governor and legislative leaders. PEBA manages retirement plans for more than six hundred thousand people. PEBA also offers various insurance products for state employees and participants, including health and life insurance.

Department of Revenue

The director is appointed by the governor, confirmed by the Senate, and considered part of the governor's cabinet. The department administers the revenue- and tax-related laws of the state, collecting 95 percent of the state's general fund revenue annually. It also administers retail sales licenses and alcoholic beverage licenses. The Department of Revenue has historically been viewed as a highly efficient operation with excellent professional leadership and staff.

Rural Infrastructure Authority

The authority is chaired by the secretary of commerce, and selection of its other members is apportioned between leaders of the General Assembly and the governor. The authority administers grants for rural water and sewer providers.

Law Enforcement

A core function of any government is the enforcement of its laws and the maintenance of order and stability within its jurisdiction. The duties include the enforcement of state laws, incarceration, and rehabilitation.

Department of Corrections

The director is appointed by the governor, confirmed by the Senate, and considered part of the governor's cabinet. The Department of Corrections houses and provides services to inmates convicted of felonies and administers the death penalty. In recent years the department's inmate count has shrunk dramatically as crime decreased in the state and drug sentences have become more targeted, allowing a number of prisons to be closed. This inmate decrease occurred even while the overall population of the state skyrocketed. According to the department's website, the inmate population in 2009 exceeded 24,000 people, and by 2022 it was reduced to less than 16,000.

Department of Juvenile Justice

The director is appointed by the governor, confirmed by the Senate, and considered part of the governor's cabinet. The Department of Juvenile Justice (DJJ) is responsible for providing custodial care and rehabilitation for children who are incarcerated in its facilities; on probation or parole; or in community placement for a criminal or status offense, such as truancy. The DJJ also provides a variety of prevention and intervention programs for at-risk youth. The DJJ has been plagued with violence in its facilities, lack of control, and legal challenges during much of its operations in the last forty years.[12]

State Law Enforcement Division

The director is appointed by the governor, confirmed by the Senate, and considered part of the governor's cabinet. The State Law Enforcement Division (SLED) is considered the state's premier investigatory agency, analogous in some ways to the FBI. The primary mission of SLED is to provide quality personnel and technical assistance to local law enforcement agencies and to conduct investigations on behalf of the state as directed by the governor and attorney general. It has carried out notable investigations of criminal gangs, human trafficking, and political corruption.

Board of Paroles and Pardons

This quasi-judicial seven-member board is appointed by the governor with the advice and consent of the Senate. The board grants or denies pardons and paroles and has the sole power to do so. In 1949, after a history of scandal, a constitutional amendment was passed restricting the governor's powers of pardon and clemency and limiting governors to granting reprieves and commutations of death sentences.

Department of Probation, Parole, and Pardon Services

The director is appointed by the governor, confirmed by the Senate, and considered part of the governor's cabinet. The department provides community supervision of criminal offenders placed on probation by a court or paroled by the State Board of Paroles and Pardons. In recent years the department has made increasing use of remote monitoring technology of sex offenders and other offenders.

Department of Public Safety

The director is appointed by the governor, confirmed by the Senate, and considered part of the governor's cabinet. The Department of Public Safety includes the Highway Patrol, State Transport Police, Bureau of Protective Services, Office of Highway Safety and Justice Programs, and the South Carolina Law Enforcement Officers Hall of Fame. It provides highway patrols, accident investigations, statehouse protection, trucking compliance, and other services. Perhaps no other state governmental officers are as well-known and as highly visible as the Highway Patrol.

Social Services

Like most states, South Carolina has numerous state agencies that provide direct social services to the public to ameliorate physical and social problems facing its citizens. From drug and alcohol treatment to children's protective services to training for the blind and deaf to the provision of health care, South Carolina has specific agencies focused on the multitude of challenges faced in a complex society.

Department of Alcohol and Other Drug Abuse Services

The director is appointed by the governor, confirmed by the Senate, and considered part of the governor's cabinet. The department is tasked with remedying the state's drug and alcohol dependency problems. The department contracts with county alcohol and drug abuse authorities to provide most of the direct prevention, treatment, and recovery services to the citizens of South Carolina. Department of Alcohol and Other Drug Abuse Services delivers almost all of its services through partnerships with county drug and alcohol treatment agencies and is therefore highly dependent on success at the local level.

Commission for the Blind

The commission is appointed by the governor and confirmed by the Senate. The commission hires a director. The commission provides specialized services, including vocational and independent living assistance, to South Carolinians who are blind or have a significant visual impairment.

Department of Consumer Affairs

Four commission members are appointed by the governor and confirmed by the Senate; four commission members are elected by the General Assembly. The department assists consumers in matters relating to unfair business and trade practices. The commission hires its director and is charged with protecting and educating consumers regarding unfair trade practices. The department tends to be an afterthought by policy makers in the state and operates on a very small budget.

Department of Disabilities and Special Needs

The commission is appointed by the governor and confirmed by the Senate. The commission hires a director. The agency plans, develops, oversees, and funds services for South Carolinians with severe, lifelong disabilities, including intellectual disability, autism, traumatic brain injury, and spinal cord injury. The agency also contracts with local providers who operate group homes for some of its clients.

Department of Employment and Workforce

The director is appointed by the governor and confirmed by the Senate. The department is responsible for unemployment benefits, workforce training, and other related services. Many citizens turn to the department in times of economic uncertainty as it administers the unemployment payments they rely on while looking for work.

Department of Health and Human Services

The director is appointed by the governor, confirmed by the Senate, and considered part of the governor's cabinet. The department's overriding mission is the delivery of Medicaid services to eligible citizens of South Carolina and coordination between health care providers, private health care management companies, and patients. The Department of Health and Human Services is a giant money-moving machine that allocates millions of dollars to Medicaid management companies, hospitals, and other health care providers.

State Housing Authority

The commission is appointed by the governor. The commission hires a director. The agency's mission is to create quality affordable housing opportunities for the state's citizens. It administers state and federal housing programs. The authority quietly operates somewhat independently from political and public view.

Human Affairs Commission

The commission is appointed by the governor with the advice and consent of the Senate, and the commission hires the agency's leadership. The South Carolina Human Affairs Commission was established in 1972 by the General Assembly at the urging of Governor John Carl West of Camden to encourage fair treatment, eliminate and prevent unlawful discrimination, and foster mutual understanding and respect among all people in this state. The General Assembly has declared that the practice of discrimination within the state because of a person's race, religion, color, sex, age, national origin, familial status, or disability to be unlawful and in conflict with the ideals of the State of South Carolina and the nation. The commission is tasked with enforcing these provisions through the enforcement of the South Carolina Human Affairs Law, the South Carolina Fair Housing Law, and the South Carolina Equal Enjoyment and Privileges to Public Accommodations Law. While the agency has significant powers, its staff is minimal, and recent governors have frequently left the commission positions unfilled.

Department of Mental Health

The commission is appointed by the governor and confirmed by the Senate. The commission hires a director. The commission provides treatment and services to citizens with mental illnesses. It uses a network of community mental health centers, clinics, hospitals, and nursing homes to provide medical and support services for the mentally ill. Battles emerge regularly about whether to combine the department with other health agencies or leave it independent as most mental-health advocates desire.

Commission for Minority Affairs

The commission is appointed by the governor with the advice and consent of the Senate. The commission hires a director. The commission is charged with studying the causes and effects of the socioeconomic deprivation of minorities in the state and implementing programs necessary to address such inequalities. The commission has been neglected by the General Assembly and governors in recent times.

Department of Public Health

Commission members are appointed by the governor and confirmed by the Senate. The commission hires a director who runs the agency. Until 2024, public health was part of the very large Department of Health and Environmental Control. In that year environmental services were carved out of its mission, and the remaining health agency was renamed. It continues to provide a multitude of services including health code administration, infectious disease control, and nursing home safety.[13]

Department of Social Services

The director is appointed by the governor, confirmed by the Senate, and considered part of the governor's cabinet. This agency promotes the safety and well-being of children and vulnerable adults. These responsibilities include protecting abused and neglected children and vulnerable adults. DSS also administers poverty reduction programs such as SNAP and TANF benefits, for which over 10 percent of South Carolinian's are eligible. During the last twenty years the Department of Social Services has seen innumerable leadership changes, public scandals involving abuse of children under its care, high turnover of staff, and a frequent lack of attention by governors' offices.[14]

Department of Vocational Rehabilitation

The commission is appointed by the governor and the Senate. The commission hires a director. The department operates highly respected vocational rehabilitation facilities across the state that are open without charge to citizens seeking confirmed workforce skill development after debilitating injuries. The agency has managed to quietly operate very efficiently for years with little intervention from the General Assembly or governors.

Workers' Compensation Commission

Commissioners are appointed by the governor and confirmed by the Senate. Commissioners hire a director. Commissioners occupy a quasijudicial role deciding workers' compensation injury cases and make decisions relating to the agency; these positions are highly sought after by interested applicants who may or may not be attorneys. The agency manages the workers' compensation system and also investigates allegations of fraud or abuse.

Other Agencies and Commissions

The State of South Carolina has numerous other smaller agencies, boards, schools, and commissions that operate for specific purposes. Some of these entities stand alone, while others are organized within larger agencies. A complete listing would be difficult in a book of this size. However included among these are the Children's Trust Fund, the School for Deaf and Blind, the Tuition Grants Commission, the Holocaust Council, the Jobs-Economic Development Authority, the Governors Schools, Wil Lou Gray Opportunity School, and the State Research Authority.

Women in State Agencies

The percentage of state elected officials in South Carolina who are women trails that of most other states. However women are well represented in the senior ranks of state agencies. At the time of the writing of this book many of the state agencies in South Carolina were led by highly effective women, including Christy Hall at the Department of Transportation, Peggy Boykin at the Public Employee

Benefit Authority, L. Eden Hendrick at Juvenile Justice, Marcia Adams at the Department of Administration, Sara Goldsby at Alcohol and Other Drug Abuse, Emily Farr at Labor, and Nanette Edwards at the Office of Regulatory Staff. While women have played an important role in state government for decades, the emergence of a large contingent of women at the highest levels of state agencies is a relatively recent phenomenon.

6

Local Governments
A New Story for South Carolina

For the most part strong local governments in South Carolina are a relatively new phenomenon. As discussed earlier in this book South Carolina from its very early days as a colony vested power in the state government, and state government controlled and continues to control many local functions. The creation of real county governments only occurred in the late twentieth century. In this chapter we will examine the growth and existence of counties, cities, and other forms of local government. Before becoming a state, South Carolina experimented with many local governance structures. One of those that survived and ultimately thrived was city government. And one leader of South Carolina's oldest city rose head and shoulders above other local leaders who came before and after.

Joseph P. Riley Jr., South Carolina's Mayor

South Carolina is populated by many species of local governmental officials: sheriffs, county council chairs, probate judges, school board members, coroners, and more.[1] Many of these positions wield formidable powers that directly affect the day-to-day lives of citizens. But for whatever reason the highest profile local officials in South Carolina tend to be mayors. In modern times mayors like Knox White of Greenville have been at the forefront of redeveloping downtowns in cooperation with the private sector to create destinations for living, working, and playing. Mayors such as Steve Benjamin in Columbia and Alfred Mae Drakeford in Camden made history by becoming the first African American mayors of their

FIGURE 7. *Charleston Mayor Joe Riley, 1986. Photograph by Jeff Amberg. Copyright © The State Media Company. All rights reserved. For more information, contact the Walker Local and Family History Center at Richland Library, Columbia, SC 29201.*

respective cities, while providing modern and effective leadership for their communities. But the recognized "king of mayors," the "granddaddy of them all," "South Carolina's mayor" is Mayor Joe Riley of Charleston who was elected in 1975 and served in that role until 2016.

Like many influential figures in the state Mayor Riley got his political start in the state House of Representatives. Elected in 1968, Riley served during a tumultuous period of racial and economic turmoil and progress. In his community he was a contradiction of sorts: an Irish Catholic in an overwhelmingly Protestant city, a supporter of civil rights who was a direct descendant of a Confederate soldier, a preacher of racial unity when campaigns in the South tended to be fought over who supported segregation the most. Riley quickly joined hands in the legislature with a group of White progressives, called the "Young Turks,"[2] and three newly elected African Americans who had broken the legislative color barrier for the first time in generations.³

Although not quite part of the Charleston aristocracy, Riley and his family were steeped in its traditions, including being a graduate of the Citadel. But Riley was never a political conformist. Riley's six years in the General Assembly were marked by his willingness to stand up to the powerful Speaker of the House Sol Blatt (discussed in chapter 2) on issues involving race, integration, and public education. Riley quickly picked up the derogatory nickname "LBJ" or "Little Black Joe" because of his commitment to civil rights and his friendships with Black elected officials and community members. After six years Representative Joe Riley had had enough of the grueling travel to and overnights in Columbia. He disliked being away from his young family. After only six years, this up-and-coming political force announced the end of his legislative career in 1974. Riley decided not to seek reelection and instead wanted to focus on building his professional legal career and his family.

Riley's planned hiatus from politics and government did not last long. In January 1975, the incumbent mayor of Charleston announced he was not seeking reelection, and with the encouragement of many friends and supporters Riley announced for mayor in February. The voters would agree and elect him to serve for more than forty years as mayor. In many ways Mayor Riley's tenure coincided with and he played a key role in massive changes in South Carolina. His leadership reasserted Charleston as the vibrant, leading city of South Carolina after years of its existence in a kind of decaying, historical netherworld.

Riley's intense focus on improving the quality of life in Charleston included robust government involvement in shaping the economic and cultural landscape of the city. His vision and efforts led to the creation of a revitalized downtown commercial sector, many new parks and recreation areas near or adjoining the waterfront, the South Carolina Aquarium, the Spoleto Arts Festival, and in his final years in office the International African American Museum. Riley's emphasis on cultural heritage and historical preservation nurtured a now thriving arts, entrepreneurial, and tourism community. Charleston attracts many more young professionals than any other city in South Carolina and has more than doubled its population since Riley first took office.[4] It has been named the number one tourist destination in the United States by Condé Nast many times.

Riley's tenure was also marked by the ancient, self-imposed tragedy that has haunted South Carolina since its Colonial time: its racial divide. In 2000 Riley led the march from Charleston to Columbia to help a growing effort to remove the Confederate flag from the statehouse dome. Because of the threat of physical violence Riley wore a heavy Kevlar vest as he set out from Charleston leading hundreds of marchers. Riley developed huge blood blisters in both feet along the route and was forced to wrap them in gauze and elevate them at every stop to continue. Entering Columbia with hundreds of supporters Riley and his group finally reached the statehouse where they were met by Governor Jim Hodges. The General Assembly voted later that year to move the Confederate flag from the dome and onto the grounds of the statehouse.

From Hurricane Hugo's fearsome wreckage to the Sofa Superstore fire that claimed the lives of nine firefighters, Mayor Riley faced historically tragic events as he led Charleston to the position of success it enjoys today. But none would equal the horror of his final year in office. In June 2015, just months before the mayor's tenure would end, a racist killer walked into Mother Emanuel African Methodist Episcopal Church and murdered its pastor along with eight church members. The pastor, Clementa Pinckney, was also a Democratic state senator, the mayor's friend, and this author's Senate seatmate.

In the weeks before the shooting, Riley had spent time working with Pinckney and other state senators advocating funding in the state's budget for the International African American Museum. In the weeks following the shooting a tearful mayor would calm his anxious city, lift up the families of the victims, and join with legislators advocating the removal of the Confederate flag from the statehouse grounds. After a fierce public and legislative debate the Confederate flag was removed later that summer.[5] Instead of coasting into retirement Riley spent his final year in office doing what he always did: leading his city through crises, planning for a better future, and creating a vision of success.

County Governments

For most of its history South Carolina had little in the way of local governments. During the colonial and post-Revolutionary eras, the state's most important subdivisions were judicial districts, as judicial administration and law enforcement were some of the only services provided to local communities by the colony and then the state. More comprehensive county boundaries were created after the American Revolution, but political power did not flow through them. As part of the progressive Constitution of 1868, the Reconstruction state government for the first time created counties as politically empowered entities. Indeed this constitutional effort shepherded a temporary revolution in the traditional South Carolina system of state power by devolving some power onto local communities. The 1868 Constitution allowed for the creation of boards of county commissioners for each county that could tax and spend, albeit for limited "county purposes."

This movement toward local empowerment was short lived. In the 1890s, the White reform backlash against Reconstruction policies resulted in the repeal of the constitutional provisions empowering counties. The job was finished by the Tillmanites in the 1896 Constitution, which, while recognizing the existence of counties, severely restricted their powers to only providing for roads, schools, ferries, bridges, and public buildings. The positions of county commissioners were done away with and their powers supplanted by the local "legislative delegations." Until the local government reforms of the 1970s, counties existed only to provide the limited functions allowed by the Tillmanites, and most had no governing bodies. Counties were absolute creatures of the state with very limited functions.

During this long period the counties were mostly governed by the General Assembly through the legislative delegation: the locally elected senator and House members. The delegation created and passed a "supply bill" each year to provide for funding of county obligations and budgets. Local senators, one from each county, were especially powerful in the local community in determining expenditures and taxation.

In the 1940s, legislators began to loosen their grip on local governance. In the late 1940s, Charleston County legislators led the devolution in power by creating a local county council and administrator. Other local delegations, including that of Kershaw County, created county governments as the century progressed.

In the progressive atmosphere of the 1960s and early '70s, the local government movement rushed forward full bore, embodied by the "West Committee," so named for its chair, Senator John Carl West[6] of Kershaw County, who would later become governor. West was a White moderate on racial issues who had his life threatened by the Ku Klux Klan. The West Committee recommended numerous constitutional changes, including those that would empower local counties, summed up in the concept of home rule. The West Committee's home rule proposals would eventually prevail, becoming law through statutory and constitutional changes in the early and mid-1970s.

Article VIII of the South Carolina Constitution limits the number of counties to forty-six. Article VII, Section 7 now forms the basis of the existence and operations of county governments. It, along with a statutory framework, allows for four types of county governments: (1) the council form, (2) the council-supervisor form, (3) the council-administrator form, and (4) the council-manager form. The different forms primarily allow for varying power-sharing structures between the county council and the county executive. Most counties selected the council-administrator form, which allows for the hiring of the county administrator by the county council. The county administrator serves as the chief administrative officer of the county while the county council performs traditional policy and rule-making roles.

During the slow development of county powers came the more rapid creation of local county officeholders. Without local unified governments and the resulting power vacuum during most of its history, the state created countywide, separately elected officials to meet the needs of the local areas. These included offices mandated by the constitution: clerk of court, coroner, and sheriff, as well as offices statutorily created: auditor, treasurer, and probate judge. Because these offices were established before the creation of local unified government, they are independently elected in partisan elections and are more or less self-governing. However since the local government reforms of the 1970s these independently elected offices are mostly reliant on the county council for funding.

While counties may no longer be "absolute" creatures of the state, they are still clearly subdivisions of the state and still reliant in large part on the General Assembly for the powers and revenue streams necessary to operate county governments. Counties in South Carolina now operate under limited home rule. Counties have been granted authority to impose limited taxes and to provide local services such as waste disposal, planning and zoning, law enforcement, recreation, public health, public libraries, and the creation of necessary boards and commissions. Counties may also, subject to a local referendum, construct and operate water, sewer, transportation, and other utilities.

County taxing authority and revenues remain highly dependent on state government. Counties may not impose taxes unless authorized by the General Assembly. The State then reciprocally provides some funding for counties through the local government fund. Further complicating the taxing and budgeting authority of local governments, the General Assembly and governor approved a severe distortion on local government property tax levies in 2006, which has proved disruptive to real estate markets, burdensome on small business, and detrimental to local education funding. Act 388 capped the reassessment of properties and shifted school operating expenses from homeowners' property taxes to business owners' property taxes, coupled with an increased state sales tax. These changes have increased costs on small businesses, destabilized education funding, cut taxes on existing homeowners, and increased taxes on new home buyers. Property taxes on owner-occupied homes are still used for bonded indebtedness purposes but not for school operating expenses.

Cities

Political power in South Carolina cities predates the existence of the state itself. Most notable is the City of Charleston, which was founded alongside the colony and long served as the focal point of the Carolinas. In the colonial period other important cities were created by the colonists and chartered by England, including the coastal cities of Beaufort and Georgetown. Early on Camden became the most important and prosperous inland city of the state, in large part because it was situated upon the navigable Wateree River as far inland as a boat could reasonably go before hitting rapids.

South Carolina's independence from England brought cities under the auspices of state government and state-created rules. Basic concepts of city organization and powers then developed rather quickly. Class conflicts also intruded in the development of cities. In the 1780s, White workers opposed the incorporation of Charleston in the newly formed state, arguing that its local government would be controlled by lawyers, planters, and wealthy merchants who would oppress the working classes.

Although falling under the concept of home rule in the 1970s, cities experienced few real changes. Over time, the state formed rules that now allow cities to choose among three forms of government: (1) the council form (a.k.a. weak mayor), (2) the council-manager form (a.k.a. strong manager), and (3) the mayor-council form (a.k.a. strong mayor). These forms are similar but allow for a varying degree of a power shared between the council, the mayor, and the city manager. Most cities have chosen the mayor-council form, while most others have chosen the council form. One important distinction between city and county governments is that cities may choose to have nonpartisan elections, thus often allowing for less nationalized, partisan debates within the local decision-making process.

Cities have many of the powers allowed counties, including law enforcement, fire protection, recreation, parks, roads, waste collection, and other utilities. Cities also have the power to create municipal criminal courts, but their jurisdiction is limited to minor offenses. Cities may not establish civil courts. Cities have the power to tax, require fees, and issue debt within restrictions prescribed by the state government.

Most cities in South Carolina offer very limited services, if any, because of their small sizes. However larger municipalities play an increasingly important role in citizens' lives due to their involvement in planning, zoning, economic development, road improvements, and similar activities. Large cities such as Charleston, North Charleston, Columbia, and Greenville have an outsized influence on the success of surrounding areas and the state as a whole.

School Districts

While local school districts are an extension of state power, they operate very much on the local level. As first established in the Reconstruction Constitution of 1868 and still in force today, the "General Assembly shall provide for the maintenance and support of a system of free public schools open to all children in the State and shall establish, organize, and support such other public institutions of learning as may be desirable" (South Carolina Constitution, Article XI, Section 3). It is a long-established, core function for the State of South Carolina to provide free public education to its children. Public education is the largest local and state expenditure in South Carolina. The state performs this obligation through a mixture of state-directed funding and policies, executed largely by locally elected school boards.

School districts are governed by constitutional and statutory requirements that have been developing since Reconstruction. Unlike cities and counties, school districts were often established separately over generations through local legislation as school districts came into existence and were combined with others. Districts therefore have a hodgepodge of governance methods. In the mid-1900s South Carolina had over fifteen hundred very small local school districts. These districts have been combined and consolidated into larger units over the years, and the state now has less than eighty traditional, local school districts. While many districts follow county borders, many counties have multiple districts within them, and some districts span county boundaries.

All school districts are governed by school boards, but the selection of the board members varies due to the local nature of the legislation that created them. Most districts now directly elect school board members in nonpartisan general elections. Some school boards have fiscal autonomy to raise property taxes and pass their budgets, while others must get approval from county councils. Local legislative delegations still have the authority to set the pay, draw the district boundaries, and set the number of board members for many districts. School boards operate within strict restraints set by state government. Much of education funding comes directly from the state and is required to be spent as directed by the state. School districts do have specific local fundings sources that provide a large portion of their operating expenses and almost all capital expenses. These local sources are primarily property taxes and fees. The state sets rules and regulations within which the school district must operate, including the size of school campuses, teacher qualifications, minimum teacher pay, curriculum, and number of school days.

Special-Purpose Districts

Because of the late emergence of county-level governments, local needs often went unmet in South Carolina. The General Assembly met this services vacuum through the patchwork creation of special-purpose districts. Special-purpose districts are governmental entities created by the state on the regional or local level. Numerous special-purpose districts exist in the state, including districts that provide water, sewer, fire, recreation, health, and other needs.

Most special-purpose districts were created individually by enabling legislation. Usually a need was brought to the attention of a local legislative delegation. The delegation would then introduce legislation setting forth the makeup and powers of a special-purpose district to meet that need. Other members of the General Assembly would defer to the local delegation on such local legislation. Enabling legislation was often amended numerous times over many years, to meet changing needs.

After the enactment of home rule in the 1970s, needs that had traditionally been met by the creation of special-purpose districts were able to be met by county governments. The creation of new single-county special-purpose districts by special legislation was prohibited. The principles of home rule have resulted in numerous debates and court cases about whether and in which situations the General Assembly may change existing special-purpose districts. Home rule also empowered county governments with limited authority to make limited changes over some special-purpose districts.

The creation of special-purpose districts is now allowed under general statutory law by an authorized vote within the proposed district area. The popular vote then determines whether the special-purpose district is created under the parameters set forth in the petition to create the district. The future of special-purpose districts in South Carolina is cloudy. Their powers, the power of the General Assembly over them, and the counties' roles continue to be fleshed out, litigated, and changed through legislation.

Excepting a few city governments, the General Assembly dominated local government for most of South Carolina's history. The local state senator, with the assistance of the House members, dictated the local budget, education policy, and county governance. With the emergence of home rule in the 1970s, county governments became a real force and opportunity for local citizens to participate. While counties' influence continues to grow, the debates about appropriate power sharing between the state and counties also continue. The urbanization of the state's population has made the importance and influence of active city governments continue to increase.

Conclusion

A Continuing Journey

South Carolina's history is intertwined with the history of the United States and of the world—from Europe to the Caribbean to Africa and beyond. For better and for worse its rich cultural milieu, its tumultuous racial history, its distrust of individual political power, and its deeply historical institutions have created a dynamic political and social culture that far outweighs in effects its relatively small size. Historically and into today South Carolina's political figures and governmental actions reverberate far outside its borders. Yet the state's internal governmental structure and workings are strangely ignored by many, excepting a few of the elected and appointed officials who make it all work. Profound changes have occurred over the last fifty years, including the emergence of a robust and powerful governor's office, consolidation of statewide elected positions, a rebalancing of legislative and executive powers, the thriving of active local governments, and much more. My hope is that this short book can help part the veil of ignorance that so often surrounds our state government's evolution, workings, and future. In the end the government we get is simply a reflection of the people we are.

APPENDIX

State Agencies

Agency	Governor appoints director	Governor appoints board or commission	Legislature appoints board or commission
State Accident Fund	Yes	No	No
Division of Aeronautics	No	Yes	No
Department of Aging	Yes	No	No
Department of Agriculture[a]	No	No	No
Department of Alcohol and Other Drug Abuse Services	Yes	No	No
Department of Archives and History	No	Yes	No
Arts Commission	No	Yes	No

Agency	Governor appoints director	Governor appoints board or commission	Legislature appoints board or commission
Office of the Commissioner of Banking and Board of Financial Institutions	No	Yes	No
Commission for the Blind	No	Yes	No
Department of Children's Advocacy	Yes	No	No
Department of Commerce	Yes	No	No
Confederate Relic Room and Military Museum	No	Yes	Yes
Conservation Bank	No	Yes	Yes
Department of Consumer Affairs	No	Yes	Yes
School for Deaf and Blind	No	Yes	No
Department of Disabilities and Special Needs	No	Yes	No
State Board of Education	No	Yes	Yes

Appendix

Agency	Governor appoints director	Governor appoints board or commission	Legislature appoints board or commission
State Department of Education[b]	No	No	No
Education Oversight Committee	No	Yes	Yes
Educational Television Commission	No	Yes	No
Election Commission	No	Yes	No
Department of Employment and Workforce	Yes	No	No
Department of Environmental Services	Yes	No	No
Ethics Commission	No	Yes	Yes
First Steps Board of Trustees	No	Yes	Yes
State Fiscal Accountability Authority[c]	No	No	No
Forestry Commission	No	Yes	No
Governors' Schools	No	Yes	No

Appendix

Agency	Governor appoints director	Governor appoints board or commission	Legislature appoints board or commission
Department of Health and Human Services	Yes	No	No
Commission of Higher Education	No	Yes	Yes
State Housing Authority	No	Yes	No
Human Affairs Commission	Yes	No	No
Commission of Indigent Defense	No	Yes	Yes
Office of Inspector General	Yes	No	No
Department of Insurance	Yes	No	No
Department of Juvenile Justice	Yes	No	No
Department of Labor, Licensing, and Regulation	Yes	No	No
State Law Enforcement Division	Yes	No	No
State Library	No	Yes	No
Lottery Commission	No	Yes	Yes

Appendix

Agency	Governor appoints director	Governor appoints board or commission	Legislature appoints board or commission
Department of Mental Health	No	Yes	No
Commission for Minority Affairs	No	Yes	No
Department of Motor Vehicles	Yes	No	No
State Museum	No	Yes	No
Department of Natural Resources	No	Yes	No
Department of Parks, Recreation, and Tourism	Yes	No	No
Board of Paroles and Pardon	No	Yes	No
Patriots Point Development Authority	No	Yes	Yes
Ports Authority	No	Yes	No
Department of Probation, Pardon, and Parole	Yes	No	No
Procurement Review Panel	No	Yes	No

Appendix

Agency	Governor appoints director	Governor appoints board or commission	Legislature appoints board or commission
Public Employee Benefit Authority	No	Yes	Yes
Department of Public Health	No	Yes	No
Department of Public Safety	Yes	No	No
Public Service Authority	No	Yes	No
Public Service Commission	No	No	Yes
Office of Regulatory Staff	Yes	No	No
SC Jobs: Economic Development Authority	No	Yes	No
SC Research Authority	No	Yes	Yes
Department of Revenue	Yes	No	No
Revenue and Fiscal Affairs Office	No	Yes	Yes
Rural Infrastructure Authority	No	Yes	Yes

Agency	Governor appoints director	Governor appoints board or commission	Legislature appoints board or commission
Department of Transportation[d]	No	Yes	No
Transportation Infrastructure Bank	No	Yes	Yes
Department of Veterans Affairs	Yes	No	No
Department of Vocational Rehabilitation	No	Yes	No
Will Lou Gray School	No	Yes	Yes
Workers' Compensation Commission	No	Yes	No

[a]The Department of Agriculture is led by the elected agriculture commissioner.

[b]The Department of Education is led by the elected superintendent of education.

[c]The State Fiscal Accountability Authority Board consists of the governor, treasurer, comptroller general, chair of Ways and Means Committee, and the chair of the Senate Finance Committee. The Commission hires the agency director.

[d]The Department of Transportation appointments are made by the governor with approval from the legislators for each district.

NOTES

Chapter 1: A Very Short History

1. Edgar, *South Carolina*, 11–16; Wallace, *Short History*, 5–14.
2. Edgar, *South Carolina*, 22.
3. Edgar, *South Carolina*, 23–24.
4. Wallace, *Short History*, 23–26.
5. Edgar, ed., *South Carolina Encyclopedia*, 346–48.
6. Edgar, ed., *South Carolina Encyclopedia*, 346–48.
7. Edgar, *South Carolina*, 82–85.
8. Edgar, ed., *South Carolina Encyclopedia*, 346–48.
9. Edgar, ed., *South Carolina Encyclopedia*, 346–48.
10. Edgar, *South Carolina*, 83.
11. Edgar, *South Carolina*, 83.
12. Edgar, ed., *South Carolina Encyclopedia*, 75, 88.
13. Wallace, *Short History*, 99–105.
14. Wallace, *Short History*, 101.
15. Booraem, *Young Hickory*, 1–5; Coit, *John C. Calhoun*, 3.
16. Edgar, ed., *South Carolina Encyclopedia*, 784–85.
17. Edgar, ed., *South Carolina Encyclopedia*, 784.
18. Edgar, *South Carolina*, 226–27.
19. Edgar, *South Carolina*, 252.
20. Edgar, ed., *South Carolina Encyclopedia*, 216–17.
21. Edgar, ed., *South Carolina Encyclopedia*, 744.
22. To learn more, see Hoffer, Peter Charles, *Cry Liberty: The Great Stono River Slave Rebellion of 1739*. Oxford University Press, 2011; and Kytle, Ethan J., and Roberts, Blain, *Denmark Vesey's Garden: Slavery and Memory in the Cradle of the Confederacy*. New Press, 2019.
23. Edgar, *South Carolina*, 275–76.
24. Kilead and Yeager, *Andrew Jackson*.
25. Edgar, *South Carolina*, 275–76.
26. Sandburg, *Abraham Lincoln*, 208–9.
27. Coit, *John C. Calhoun*, 212–13.
28. Edgar, *South Carolina*, 383.

29. Edgar, ed., *South Carolina Encyclopedia*, 217.
30. Edgar, *South Carolina*, 386.
31. Edgar, ed., *South Carolina Encyclopedia*, 217.
32. Edgar, *South Carolina*, 393.
33. Edgar, *South Carolina*, 386.
34. Zuczek, *State of Rebellion*.
35. Zuczek, *State of Rebellion*, 35, 53.
36. Zuczek, *State of Rebellion*, 55–56, 73.
37. Zuczek, *State of Rebellion*, 88–105.
38. Edgar, *South Carolina*, 402.
39. Zuczek, *State of Rebellion*, 188–89.
40. Edgar, *South Carolina*, 405.
41. Zuczek, *State of Rebellion*, 201.
42. The antebellum elite has been referred to as the Conservatives or Bourbon Democrats, hearkening back to the French aristocracy and the Southern whiskey.
43. Cooper, *Conservative Regime*.
44. Wallace, *Short History*, 623–24; Edgar, *South Carolina*, 434–43.
45. Clyburn, *Blessed Experiences*.

Chapter 2: The Legislative Branch

1. The information in this profile is drawn from the following sources: Gates, Jr., *African Americans*; Edgar, ed. *South Carolina Encyclopedia*, 881–82; *Post and Courier*, "Different Kind of Statehouse Monument Honors 'Someone we can all love,'" July 22, 2024.
2. The information in this profile is drawn from the following sources: Cauthen, *Speaker Blatt*; Edgar, ed., *South Carolina Encyclopedia*, 78–79.
3. The Blatts were not the only Jewish, Eastern European family to thrive in rural South Carolina. The Morris Ness family similarly immigrated from Poland and ultimately settled in Denmark, South Carolina. Morris and Raye Levy Ness ran a dry goods store there and had five children, among them Julius "Bubba" Ness. As a teenager Bubba Ness would meet Speaker of the House Sol Blatt, fight in World War II, practice law in his rural community, be elected to the General Assembly, and eventually serve as chief justice of the South Carolina Supreme Court. Bubba Ness was famous in South Carolina legal circles for his gruff but kind manner and his love of family, friends, and life.
4. Edgar, ed., *South Carolina Encyclopedia*, 643
5. Wallace, *Short History*, 251–52.
6. Wallace, *Short History*, 271–73.
7. Edgar, ed., *South Carolina Encyclopedia*, 216.
8. Edgar, ed., *South Carolina Encyclopedia*, 216.

9. Carter and Young, *South Carolina Governor*, 32.
10. Seifter, *Gubernatorial Administration*, 483.
11. *Reynolds v. Sims*, 377 U.S. 533 (1964).
12. The legislative branch did operate a sunset review effort during parts of the 1980s and 1990s under the State Reorganization Commission. The commission partnered with the Legislative Audit Council to audit, change, or delete programs that were ineffective. The commission was defunded in the late 1990s.

Chapter 3: The Executive Branch

1. Reisinger, Tyler Lang, *Beyond Beyle: Assessing the Measurement of Institutional and Informal Gubernatorial Powers*, MA thesis, Virginia Polytechnic Institute (2008); Bangcaya, Matthew, et al. *Professionalization and Effectiveness in State Legislatures* (Texas A&M Bush School of Government and Public Service, May 2015).
2. "Republicans are Making a Weak NC Governor's Office Even Weaker," *Raleigh News and Observer*, December 31, 2023.
3. The information in this profile is drawn from the following sources: Edgar, ed., *South Carolina Encyclopedia*, 961–62; Edgar, *South Carolina*, 432–52; Wallace, *Short History*, 614–71.
4. Edgar, *South Carolina*, 433.
5. Edgar, *South Carolina*, 438.
6. Edgar, *South Carolina*, 443.
7. The information in this profile is drawn from Edgar, ed., *South Carolina Encyclopedia*, 803–4.
8. For further information on the Young Turks please see the discussion of Mayor Joseph Riley in the Local Government section of this book (chapter 6).
9. Edgar, ed., *South Carolina Encyclopedia*, 803.
10. Edgar, ed., *South Carolina Encyclopedia*, 845–46.
11. Edgar, ed., *South Carolina Encyclopedia*, 386–87.
12. Edgar, ed., *South Carolina Encyclopedia*, 217; Zuczek, *State of Rebellion*, 15–16.
13. Edgar, ed., *South Carolina Encyclopedia*, 217.
14. Edgar, *South Carolina*, 386.
15. See, e.g., Zuczek, *State of Rebellion*.
16. Edgar, ed., *South Carolina Encyclopedia*, 217.
17. Edgar, *South Carolina*, 438.
18. Carter and Young, *South Carolina Governor*.
19. Edgar, ed., *South Carolina Encyclopedia*, 218.
20. Edgar, ed., *South Carolina Encyclopedia*, 218.
21. Seifter, *Gubernatorial Administration*, 131, 483.

22. See Tyler Reisinger, *Beyond Beyle*. VDM Verlag, 2009.
23. See Tyler Reisinger, *Beyond Beyle*. VDM Verlag, 2009.
24. Edgar, ed., *South Carolina Encyclopedia*, 979.
25. *State ex rel. Daniel v. Broad River Power Co.*, 153 S.E. 537, 560 (S.C. 1929).
26. "After Failed Referendum, SC Lawmakers Unlikely to Try Appointing the Superintendent," *Post and Courier*, December 23, 2018.
27. Wallace, *Short History*, 113–14.
28. Wallace, *Short History*, 583–85, 594.
29. During a brief period of competitive partisan elections in South Carolina, Democrat Nick Theodore served as lieutenant governor while Republican Carroll Campbell served as governor. Similarly, Republican Bob Peeler was lieutenant governor under Democratic governor Jim Hodges.

Chapter 4: The Judicial Branch

1. Because of the lack of comprehensive authority on South Carolina's judiciary and its history, the author relied on many publications, which are listed in the Works Consulted section of this book. The author is also indebted to former University of South Carolina Law School Dean Robbie Wilcox for discussion and access to his notes on South Carolina's legal history.
2. The information in this profile is drawn from the following sources: Burke Jr. and Assey, eds., *Madam Chief Justice*, Robert J. Moore, interviewer, Jean Toal, interviewee, *University of South Carolina Department of Oral History*. February 21, 2003. South Carolina Judicial Department website.
3. Ernest Finney lived a groundbreaking life. Known as a peaceful but firm force for good, he became chief justice in 1994. Justice Finney graduated in 1954 from a short-lived law school program at South Carolina State University. The law school was created as part of Jim Crow era efforts to keep Blacks from attending the University of South Carolina's law school. Finney used this foundation to change South Carolina. Early in his career he practiced law in Sumter County and took on civil rights cases. He was elected in 1972 to the South Carolina House and to the circuit court bench in 1976. Bristow Marchant, "Ernest Finney, Pioneering SC Chief Justice, 'A Legitimate Hero,'" *State Newspaper*, December 5, 2017.
4. Burke Jr. and Assey, *Madam Chief Justice*, 19.
5. Burke Jr. and Assey, *Madam Chief Justice*, 19.
6. On the colonial-era court, see Wallace, *Short History*, 114–119; Edgar, ed., *South Carolina Encyclopedia*, 979–80.
7. Wallace, *Constitutional History*, 22.

8. Wright was one of the first Black attorneys in Pennsylvania who then came to South Carolina with the Freedmen's Bureau. He participated in the 1868 Constitutional Convention and was subsequently elected to the state Senate. He served there until he was elected to the state supreme court with bipartisan support. Wright was the first Black man elected to a state or federal appellate court in the United States. His written opinions were considered so astute that White detractors accused him of having a White attorney write them for him. When White power returned to the state with the election of Wade Hampton as governor, Wright angered White Democrats by refusing, in a legal opinion, to recognize Hampton as governor. Impeachment proceedings were initiated accusing Wright of drunkenness, and Wright resigned rather than face an impeachment vote. According to Wright, Wade Hampton himself told Wright that the charges against him were false, and Wright was a "pure judge."

9. Chief Justice Eugene S. Blease was elected in 1931 and was not the most senior associate justice.

10. Southern, "Beyond Jim Crow," 209–27.

11. Hays, "South Carolina's Judicial System," 207.

Chapter 5: Important State Agencies

1. The information in this profile is drawn from the following sources: Edgar, ed., *South Carolina Encyclopedia,* 508–9; Cassie Cope, "100 Years of Controversy and Potholes in South Carolina," *The State,* March 10, 2017.

2. Edgar, ed., *South Carolina Encyclopedia,* 508–9.

3. "The 1935 Mutiny at the SC Highway Department," *The State,* October 25, 2025.

4. South Carolina Department of Archives and History, *The Silver Crescent Standard* (blog), November 27, 2019.

5. "Haley Blasted on Arts, Teacher Raise Vetoes," *Post and Courier,* July 9, 2012.

6. "House Overrides First Set of Sanford Vetoes," *Post and Courier,* May 29, 2008.

7. See "NukeGate Scandal," Wikipedia.

8. "A Pat on the Back to Grooms, Sheheen for Practical Roads Bill," *Statehouse Report,* April 28, 2017.

9. "DHEC Will Split into Separate Health and Environmental Agencies," June 24, 2024, ABC4 News.

10. See, e.g., "Will 2022 be the Year for Ethics Reform in South Carolina?" *Post and Courier,* January 17, 2022.

11. The lead sponsor and drafter of this legislation was the author of this book.

12. See, e.g., "SC Department of Juvenile Justice and US Department of Justice Announce Voluntary Settlement," *Post and Courier*, April 14, 2022.

13. "DHEC Will Split into Separate Health and Environmental Agencies," June 24, 2024, ABC4 News.

14. See, e.g., "SC DSS Director Michael Leach Trying to Transform the Long Troubled Social Services Agency," *Post and Courier*, October 27, 2020.

Chapter 6: Local Governments

1. The information in this profile is drawn from the following sources: Hicks, *The Mayor*; Segrist, Liz. "Mayors Perspective: 40 Years of Changing Charleston," October 30, 2015, scbiznews.

2. The Young Turks included such luminaries as Senators Harry Chapman, Dick Riley, and Isadore Lourie. Although often fighting losing battles at the outset the Young Turks ultimately had a profound influence on the policies of the state. They became a dominant progressive force in government for more than a decade and enacted progressive policies in the areas of civil rights, consumer protections, and education reform. Their influence waned as Republican control of the state came into being. The phrase "Young Turks" originally referred to young Turkish reformers who favored replacement of the Ottoman Empire's absolute monarchy with a constitutional form of government.

3. Herbert Fielding, I. S. Leevy Johnson, and Jim Felder made history in the late 1960s by becoming the first African Americans elected since 1902. Riley was particularly close to Fielding as they both hailed from Charleston and chose to sit next to each other in the house. Demonstrating the effects of segregation well into the 1960s, Riley once reminisced that Fielding was the first Black man with whom he had ever had dinner.

4. Segrist, Liz. "Mayors Perspective: 40 Years of Changing Charleston," October 30, 2015, scbiznews.

5. This author drafted and introduced the legislation that ultimately removed the Confederate flag from the statehouse grounds and spoke with Mayor Riley the day after the murders and in weeks following about the need to properly grieve, memorialize, and remember the victims.

6. Grose, *Looking for Utopia*.

WORKS CONSULTED

Bass, Jack, and W. Scott Poole. *The Palmetto State: The Making of Modern South Carolina*. University of South Carolina Press, 2009.
Booraem, Hendrik. *Young Hickory: The Making of Andrew Jackson*. Taylor Trade, 2001.
Burke, W. Lewis, Jr., and Joan Assey, eds. *Madam Chief Justice: Jean Hoefer Toal of South Carolina*. University of South Carolina Press, 2016.
Carter, Luther F., and David S. Mann, eds. *Government in the Palmetto State: Toward the Twenty-First Century*. Institute for Public Affairs, University of South Carolina, 1992.
Carter, Luther F., and Richard D. Young. *The South Carolina Governor: The Emergence of an Institution*. Institute for Public Service and Policy Research, University of South Carolina, 2003.
Cauthen, John K. *Speaker Blatt: His Challenges Were Greater*. University of South Carolina Press, 1978.
Clyburn, James E. *Blessed Experiences*. University of South Carolina Press, 2014.
Coit, Margaret L. *John C. Calhoun: American Portrait*. University of South Carolina Press, 1991.
Cooper, William J. *The Conservative Regime: South Carolina, 1877–1890*. Johns Hopkins University Press, 1968.
Cureton, Jasper. *Coming of Age: The South Carolina Court of Appeals*. South Carolina Judicial Department.
Edgar, Walter. *South Carolina: A History*. University of South Carolina Press, 1999.
Edgar, Walter, ed. *The South Carolina Encyclopedia*. University of South Carolina Press, 2006.
Gates, Henry Louis, Jr., and Donald Yacovone. *The African Americans: Many Rivers to Cross*. Smiley Books, 2013.
Grose, Phillip G. *Looking for Utopia: The Life and Times of John C. West*. University of South Carolina Press, 2011.
Hambright, Barry Edmond. "The South Carolina Supreme Court." PhD diss., University of South Carolina, 1981.

Hays, Steven W. "South Carolina's Judicial System: Reform in a Traditionalistic Setting." *Journal of Political Science* 24, no. 1 (November 1996): 203–29.
Hicks, Brian. *The Mayor: Joe Riley and the Rise of Charleston.* Evening Post Books, 2015.
Johnson, Herbert A., ed. *South Carolia Legal History: Proceedings of the Reynolds Conference, University of South Carolina, December 2–3, 1977.* University of South Carolina Press, 1980.
Jordan, Frank E., Jr., *The Primary State: A History of the Democratic Party in South Carolina 1896–1962.* Privately printed, 1966.
Kilead, Brian, and Don Yeager. *Andrew Jackson and the Miracle of New Orleans.* Sentinel 2017.
Littlejohn, Bruce. *Littlejohn's South Carolina Judicial History: 1930–2004.* Joggling Board Press, 2005.
Meacham, Jon. *American Lion: Andrew Jackson in the White House.* Random House, 2008.
Richardson, Gail Ness, ed. *Bubba Stories.* Privately printed, 2013.
Sandburg, Carl. *Abraham Lincoln: The Prairie Years,* Harcourt, Brace & World, 1926.
Scott, Ronald T. "Judicial Selection in South Carolina: Is the Time Ripe for Systematic Restructuring and Improvement: You Be the Judge." *South Carolina Law Review* 68, no. 4 (2017).
Seifter, Miriam. "Gubernatorial Administration." *Harvard Law Review* 131, no. 2 (December 2017): 484.
Southern, David. "Beyond Jim Crow Liberalism: Judge Waring's Fight Against Segregation in South Carolina, 1942–52," *Journal of Negro History* 66, no. 3 (Fall 1981): 209–27.
Ulbrich, Holley Hewitt. *Funding Government in South Carolina.* Institute for Public Service and Policy Research, University of South Carolina, 2002.
Ulbrich, Holley Hewitt, and Ada Louise Steirer. *Local Governments and Home Rule in South Carolina: A Citizen's Guide.* Strom Thurmond Institute, 2004.
Wallace, David Duncan. *Constitutional History of South Carolina From 1725–1775.* Hugh Wilson, Printer, 1899.
Wallace, David Duncan. *South Carolina, A Short History 1520–1948.* University of North Carolina Press, 2011.
Zuczek, Richard. *State of Rebellion.* University of South Carolina Press, 1996.

INDEX

Italicized page numbers indicate pages with images.

Act 388 (2006), 119
Adams, Marcia, 111
adjutant generals, 52, 68–69
African American Heritage Commission, 94
Agency Salary Head Commission, 40, 103
agricultural commissioners, 67, 133
American Revolution, 1, 8, 49
Anglican Church/Church of England, 7
Arts Commission, 94, 127
Athletic Commission, 96

attorney generals, 13, 60–61, 62, 63, 105
Backcountry, 6–7, 8, 9, 77, 78
Banking and Investment Management Division (State Treasurer), 65
Barbados immigrants, 4, 26
Benjamin, Steve, 113
Berkeley, John, 3
Beyle, Thad, 59, 60
Black Codes, 50
Black colleges: 16, 138n3; *see also* Orangeburg Massacre
Black militias, 13
Black political power: xii, 10, 11–12, 28, 29, 50–51, 78; *see also* Legislative Black Caucus
Blackbeard, 5
Blatt, Solomon: 19, 24; Jewishness, 23, 24, 25, 136n3; racism, 25, 26;

South Carolina House of Representatives speakership, 23, 25, 115
Board of Economic Advisers, 40
Board of Paroles and Pardons, 105, 106, 131
Bonnett, Stede, 5
Bourbons, 14, 15, 44, 51, 79–80, 136n42
Boykin, Peggy, 111
Briggs v. Elliott (1951), 81
British colonial rule, 2–4, 27
Brown v. Board of Education (1954), 81
Brown, Edgar, 19, 94
Budget and Control Board, 29, 55, 103
Bureau of Protective Services, 54, 106
business community, 16, 28
Byrnes, James, 52

Cacica, 2
Caldwell-Boylston House, 59
Calhoun, John C., 6, 9–10, 19, 83
Calhoun, Patrick, 6
Campbell, Carroll, 43, 49, 52, 138n29
Catawbas, 1, 73
Cemetery Board, 96
Chamberlain, Daniel, 13, 14
Chandler, Lee, 74
Charles II, 2
Charles Town, 5, 6, 77
Chicora, 1

Chicora, Francisco de, 1
Children's Trust Fund, 57, 110
Circuit Court Act (1796), 78
city governments, 113, 120, 123
civil rights movement: xii, 16, 81, 82, 138n3; see also *Briggs v. Elliott* (1951); *Brown v. Board of Education* (1954); Clark, Septima; Clyburn, James; Newman, I. DeQuincey; Perry, Matthew
Civil War, xi, 1, 10
Clark, Septima, 16
Cleveland, Grover, 46
Clyburn, James, 16
Cofitachequi, 2
Colleton, John, 3, 4
Commission for Minority Affairs, 109, 131
Commission for the Blind, 107, 128
Commission on Higher Education, 101
Commons House of Assembly, 5, 26, 27, 76
Comptroller General's Office, 65, 66
Confederate flag removal, 116, 117, 140n5
Confederate Relic Room Commission, 94–95, 128
Conservation Bank, 33, 98, 128
Constitution of 1776, 7, 67, 77, 94
Constitution of 1790, 28, 78
Constitution of 1865, 10, 49–50
Constitution of 1868, 11, 13, 14, 50, 63, 69, 79, 80, 84, 99, 121, 139n8
Constitution of 1895, 12, 15, 22–23, 46, 51, 80
Constitution of 1896, 15, 117
Cooper, Anthony Ashley, 3
cotton, 9, 20
county commissioners, 117
county government power, 11, 29, 113, 117–20, 123
Crazy Caucus: 73, 74; *see also* Crocker, Ginger; Keyserling, Harriet; McEachin, Malloy; McFadden, Bob; Toal, Jean Hoefer

Crocker, Ginger, 73

De Soto, Hernando, 2
Debt Management Division (State Treasurer), 65
decentralized power, xi, xii, 82
Declaration of Independence, 27, 67, 68, 88
Declaration of the Causes of Secession, 10
Democratic Party: Black participation, 13, 16, 47, 81; racist history, 13, 22, 44, 46; White domination of, 10, 13, 22, 24, 44–46, 81
Department of Administration, 29, 52, 55, 56, 57, 103, 111
Department of Agriculture, 67, 127, 133
Department of Alcohol and Other Drug Abuse Services, 56, 106, 111, 127
Department of Archives & History, 94, 127
Department of Commerce, 28, 56, 96, 128
Department of Consumer Affairs, 56, 107, 128
Department of Corrections, 56, 104
Department of Disabilities and Special Needs, 107, 128
Department of Education, 63–64, 99–100, 128, 133
Department of Employment and Workforce, 107, 129
Department of Environmental Services, 56, 98, 129
Department of Health and Human Services, 56, 107–108, 129
Department of Insurance, 56, 96, 130
Department of Juvenile Justice (DJJ), 56, 105, 111, 130
Department of Labor, Licensing, and Regulation, 56, 96, 130
Department of Mental Health, 56, 108, 130

Department of Motor Vehicles, 56, 96–97, 131
Department of Natural Resources, 52, 57, 99, 131
Department of Parks, Recreation, and Tourism, 56, 99, 131
Department of Probation, Parole, and Pardon Services, 56, 105–106, 131
Department of Public Health, 56, 109, 131
Department of Public Safety, 56, 106, 132
Department of Revenue, 56, 104, 132
Department of Social Services, 28, 56, 109
Department of the Judiciary, 61
Department of Transportation, 29, 52, 57, 91–92, 94, 97, 111, 132, 133
Department of Vocational Rehabilitation, 57, 110, 133
distrust of consolidated power, 4, 5–6, 7, 8, 10, 12, 26, 49, 77, 125
Drakeford, Alfred Mae, 113

Edgar, Walter B., 10
Edgefield Agricultural Society, 44
Education Oversight Committee, 40, 129
Educational Television Commission, 100, 129
Edwards Nanette, 111
Election Commission, 102, 129
Ellington riots, 13
Employment Security Commission, 56
Eslinger, Victoria, 72
Ethics Commission, 102–3, 129

farmers' reform movement, 15, 44, 67
Farr, Emily, 111
Finney, Ernest, 73, 74, 138n3
First Steps Board of Trustees, 40, 100, 129
Forestry Commission, 56, 98, 129
Fort Johnson, 21
Fort Sumter, 10, 21, 22

Foster Care Review Boards, 57
freedom of religion, 3
French Huguenots, 2, 3, 6
Friendship Nine lunch counter protest, 16
Fundamental Constitutions of the Carolinas, 3, 26

General Assembly: 7, 13, 29, 30, 53, 59; appointment powers, 40, 43, 49, 51, 55, 61, 67, 68, 101, 104, 107; appropriation powers, 32, 54–55, 57–8; and county governance, 117–18, 119; as dominant political body, 8, 11, 26, 28, 67; and executive branch, 43, 46, 49, 51, 53, 54–55, 57–58, 59, 61, 65; and judicial branch, 77–79, 80–81, 82, 83–84, 85–86, 88–89; origins, 5–6, 7–8, 27; power sharing, 28–29, 40–41, 49; public education, 63, 64, 121; racist past, 46, 109; see also judicial branch; South Carolina House of Representatives; South Carolina Senate
German immigrants, 3, 6
Gibbes, Robert, 4
Ginsburg, Ruth Bader, 72
Goldsby, Sara, 111
Government Restructuring Act (1994), 52, 57
Government Restructuring Act (2014), 29, 34, 39, 52, 55, 57, 103
Governor's Mansion, 58, 59
Governors School for Math & Science, 110, 129
Governors School for the Arts, 110, 129
governors: agency appointment power, 43, 52, 55–57, 59; budgetary influence, 43, 53, 57–58; bully pulpit power, 43, 44, 53, 58, 69; Executive Budget Office, 53, 57; increased power of, 8, 28, 29, 43–44, 49, 60; pardon authority, 50, 52; popular

election of, 10, 11, 50; staff members, 53, 57; state militia command, 50, 52; term limits, 48, 49, 51, 52; veto power, 10, 49, 50, 54–55; *see also* lieutenant governors
gradualism, 81
Grand Council, 5, 76, 77
Gressette, Marion, 19
Guardian Ad Litem Program, 55

Haley, Nikki, 19, 38, 94
Hall, Christy, 111
Hampton, Wade, 13–15, 43, 46, 51, 79, 139n8
Hayes, Rutherford B., 13, 14
Hendrick, L. Eden, 111
Hepworth, Thomas, 76
Highway Patrol, 106
Hodges, Jim, 100, 116, 138n29
Hollings, Ernest F. "Fritz," 19, 43, 49, 52
Holocaust Council, 110
home rule, 73, 118, 119, 120, 123
Human Affairs Commission, 73, 108, 130
Hyde, Edward, 3

indentured servants, 3
Indigenous Americans: xi, 1, 2, 4–5, 26; *see also* Catawbas; Pee Dees; Waccamaws
indigo, 7
industrialization, xii, 16
International African American Museum, 116
Irish immigrants: 3; *see also* Scots-Irish immigrants

Jackson, Andrew, 6, 9–10, 83
Jews immigrants, 3, 19, 23–25, 136n3
Jim Crow. *see* segregation
Jobs-Economic Development Authority, 110
Johnson, Andrew, 10
Johnston, Olin D., 25, 92, 92–94

Joint Bond Review Committee, 33, 40
judicial branch: 71, 76, 81–82, 86, 90; circuit courts, 80, 85–86; court of appeals, 82, 83–85; court of law, 77, 79; court of equity, 77, 79; General Assembly election of judges, 78, 80–81, 88–89; Judicial Merit Selection Commission, 33, 89; magistrate/municipal courts, 86, 87; probate courts, 87, 88; unified court system, 82, 85; *see also* Circuit Court Act (1796); Constitution of 1868; Finney, Ernest; Hepworth, Thomas; South Carolina Supreme Court; Toal, Jean Hoefer; Trott, Nicholas; Wright, Jonathon Jasper

Keyserling, Harriet, 73
Kirk, Roger, 73
Ku Klux Klan, 12, 118

Lace House, 59
land ownership protections, 3, 11
Legislative Audit Council, 40, 137n12
Legislative Black Caucus, 74
lieutenant governors, 52, 68, 138n29
lobbyists, 31, 102
Locke, John, 3, 26
Lords Proprietors, 2–3, 5, 26, 49, 60, 67, 76
Lowcountry elites, 7, 8

majority Black population, 8
Manning, Richard I., 92
Marion, Francis "the Swamp Fox," 8
McEachin, Malloy, 73
McFadden, Bob, 73
McKee, Henry, 20
McKee, John, 20
McMahon, Judy Bridges, 73
McMaster, Henry, 37
McNair, Robert, 43, 49, 52
Medical Examiners Board, 96
modernization, xii, 16–17, 25, 28, 73, 74–75

Moore, James, Jr., 26, 27
Mother Emanuel African Methodist Episcopal Church murders, 116
Mulvaney, Mick, 19

National Guard, 68, 93
Newman, I. DeQuincey, 16
Nixon, Richard M., 73
nullification, 9, 83

Office of Highway Safety and Justice Programs, 106
Office of the Comptroller General, 65, 66
Office of the State Treasurer, 65
Office of Veterans Affairs, 55, 133
one-party dominance, xii, 16, 60
Orangeburg Massacre, 16

Parker, Niles, 65
Parris Island, 2
Pee Dees, 1
Peeples, Rodney A., 74
Perry, Matthew, 16
Pinckney, Clementa, 116
plantation economy system, 4, 7, 9
political corruption, 55, 62, 65, 66, 89, 105
poor Whites, 9, 93
population growth, xi, xii, 6, 15, 67, 77, 116
Ports Authority, 97, 131
Programs Division (State Treasurer), 65
public education: 11, 13, 63, 99; see also Department of Education; General Assembly: public Education
Public Employee Benefit Authority (PEBA), 103–104, 111, 131
Public Service Authority-Santee Cooper Utility, 97, 132
Public Service Commission, 40, 132

racism, 16, 25; see also Blatt, Solomon: racism; Confederate flag removal; Democratic Party: racist history; General Assembly: racist past; Ku Klux Klan; segregation; slavery; Tillman, Benjamin Ryan "Pitchfork Ben": racism; White racial violence/terrorism
Rainey, Joseph H., 11
Real Estate Commission, 96
Reconstruction: Black political power, xii, 22, 28, 50–51, 63; end of, 13; state government during, 13, 50–51, 63, 78, 79–80, 117; see also Constitution of 1868
Reconstruction Acts (1867), 11
Red Shirts, 13
Reformers, 12, 15, 51, 78, 79
Regulators, 6–7, 77
Republican Party: 22, 24, 73; ascendancy to power, xii, 29, 37; General Assembly control, 13, 29, 37, 140n2; Reconstruction-era Black dominance, 10, 11, 14, 63, 79; White voters, 10, 14, 16, 47, 63, 80
Revolution of 1719, 5, 26, 76
rice, 7
Riley, Joseph P.: 114; Catholicism, 114; Charleston mayorship, 115, 116; civil rights support, 114, 115, 116–17, 140n3,5; South Carolina House of Representatives, 114, 115
Riley, Richard "Dick": 19, 43, 47, 49, 140n2; Democratic Party, 47, 48; General Assembly service, 48, 49; see also Young Turks
Roosevelt, Franklin D., 81
royalists, 2
rural farmers, 15, 44
Rural Infrastructure Authority, 104, 132
Rutledge, John, 19, 78
Rylea, Charles, 21

Sanford, Mark, 94

Sayle, William, 49
Schlesigner, Joseph, 59
school boards, 64, 113, 121–22
school districts, 64, 99, 121–22
School for Deaf and Blind, 110, 128
Scots-Irish immigrants, 6, 9
Scott, Tim, 19
secretaries of state, 67
segregation/desegregation, 10, 12, 15, 16, 48, 81, 114, 140n3
Sesquicentennial Commission, 57
Sheheen, Robert J. "Bob," 52, 73
Sheheen, Vincent, xiii, 29, 97, 139n11, 140n5
slavery, xi, 1, 3–4, 6, 7, 8–9, 10, 49, 50
Smalls, Robert, 15, 19, 20, 20–21, 22, 23, 49, 50
South Carolina Aquarium, 115
South Carolina Equal Employment and Privileges to Public Accommodations Law, 108
South Carolina ETV, 100
South Carolina Fair Housing Law, 108
South Carolina House of Representatives, 27–28, 30–31, 33, 101, 102, 118, 123, 138n3; coalition-building, 32, 33; committee structures/various committees, 31, 32, 33, 34–35; election of judges, 32, 77–79, 80, 82, 85–86, 88–90; Legislative Ethics Committee, 34, 35, 103; Operations and Management Committee, 34, 35; Oversight Committee, 34, 35; Rules Committee, 34, 35; Speaker Pro Tempore, 33, 34; Speakership, 32, 33, 94, 98, 115; Ways and Means Committee, 32, 34, 35, 38, 103
South Carolina Human Affairs Law, 108
South Carolina Law Enforcement Officers Hall of Fame, 106
South Carolina Military Department, 68
South Carolina Opioid Recovery Fund, 103
South Carolina Provincial Congress; see General Assembly
South Carolina Senate: 27, 30–31, 36–39, 72–73; advice and consent power, 35, 52, 55, 56, 101, 105, 108, 109; blocking of bills, 36, 63; committee structure/various committees, 37, 38, 39; confirmation power, 35, 36–37, 38; election of judges, 32, 77–79, 80, 82, 85–86, 88–90; Finance Committee, 38, 39; filibuster rule, 31, 36; Judiciary Committee, 38, 39; Senate presidency, 37, 38
South Carolina Supreme Court, 50, 54–55, 73–74, 79, 136n3
Southern Strategy, 73
Spanish explorers, 1, 2
special-purpose districts, 122, 123
Spoleto Arts Festival, 115
state agency head appointments, xii, 28, 29
state auditors, 102, 103, 119
State Board of Education, 64, 100, 128
State Fiscal Accountability Authority (SFAA), 103
State Fiscal Affairs Agency, 40, 103
State Highway Commission. see Department of Transportation
State Housing Authority, 56, 108, 130
State Infrastructure Bank, 40
State Law Enforcement Division (SLED), 56, 105, 130
State Library, 95, 130
State Museum, 95, 131
State Research Authority, 110
State Transport Police, 106
state treasurers, 64–66, 103, 119, 133
state-run alcohol dispensary, 80
states' rights, 43, 83
Stono Rebellion (1739), 8
Sumter, Thomas "the Gamecock," 8

superintendents of education, 11, 60, 63–64, 100, 133

taxes: 14–15, 48, 57, 62, 96, 97, 101, 104, 117, 118; for education, 25, 63; on local services, 119, 121; on property, 119, 120, 122
Thurmond, Strom, 19, 49
Tilden, Samuel J., 13
Tillman, Benjamin Ryan "Pitchfork Ben," 19, 28, 43, 45, 46, 80; Constitution of 1895, 22–23, 46, 117; Democratic Party, 45, 46; economic populism, 44, 46, 51; as governor, 15, 45–46, 49; leveraging of Black voters, 45; racism, 15, 44, 45, 46, 51
Tillmanism, 15, 49, 80, 117
Toal, Jean Hoefer: 71, 72; as chief justice of South Carolina, 71–72, 75, 83; racial progressivism, 71, 73; South Carolina Supreme Court, 73, 74, 75
tobacco, 7
tourism, 95, 99, 116
Treasury Management Position (State Treasurer), 66
trial by jury, 3
Trott, Nicholas, 60, 76
Tuition Grants Commission, 110

Unionists, 83
United States Constitution, 8
United States Supreme Court, 31, 35–36

urbanization, 16, 123

Vesey, Denmark, 8
voter intimidation/suppression, 13, 14
voting rights: 3; for Black citizens, 11, 13, 14, 15, 49, 50; removal of property rights qualification, 10, 11, 50

Waccamaws, 1
Waring, J. Waites, 81
Washington, George, 8
Welsh immigrants, 3
West Committee, 118
West, John C., 28, 43, 52, 73, 108, 118
White conservatism, 12, 14–15, 44, 45, 46, 51, 78, 79, 80
White progressives, 114
White racial violence/terrorism: 11, 13, 14, 50; *see also* Ku Klux Klan; Red Shirts
White Reform movement, 12, 15, 51, 78, 79
White supremacy, xii, 4, 14, 16, 79, 93
White, Knox, 113
Wil Lou Gray Opportunity School, 110
Workers' Compensation Commission, 85, 110, 133
Wright, Jonas Jasper, 50, 79, 80, 139n8

Yeamans, John, 4
Young Turks, 48, 114, 140n2
Young, Richard, xii

ABOUT THE AUTHOR

Vincent Sheheen was elected mayor of Camden, South Carolina, in 2024. He served in the South Carolina Senate from 2004 to 2020, served in the South Carolina House of Representatives from 2000 to 2004, and was twice a nominee for governor. Sheheen has taught courses at the University of South Carolina Honors College, Joseph F. Rice School of Law, and Francis Marion University Non-Profit Institute. He is cohost of the podcast *Bourbon in the Back Room* and author of *The Right Way: Getting the Palmetto State Back on Track*.